I'm No Angel

(First Edition)

by

R. James Misfeldt

ISBN : (978-1-926515-38-0)

For additional information about *I'm No Angel* (and associated content), surf to :

http://abfbook.telostic.com

Table of Contents

About the author

rj misfeldt, author of fiction and plays, lives with his artist-wife on the shore of Last Mountain Lake in southern Saskatchewan, Canada.

The long cold winters offer stretches of time to write and paint. At present, he's working to finish a novel, *Benny*, who back in the fifties would have been called a "retard". He's most fascinating character, who, lacking social graces, says what he thinks and wants.

rj's compiling books of short stories and stage plays. In the radio play, *See No Evil*, a young British Home Child, who was shipped to Canada and placed on a farm by the federal government to work as slave labour, is charged with murder.

Decades before domestic violence and abuse became a topic for movies, he wrote a short story in which the abused son, coming into the highway garage with his .22 rifle, shoots his father to save his mother from being beaten up.

The story was rejected by a magazine editor because "no one could be that evil".

R. James Misfeldt

Author

Part 1

1

A cold April wind cuts through Angela's spring coat as she waits on the station platform for Mr Cox. He did say on the phone that he would pick her up. But she's left stranded. Not a good omen.

What if she got off at the wrong town? No, thank God. Paradise Junction is painted on the grain elevator.

Not a soul on Main Street. The false-fronted shops closed for the night as the shopkeepers have gone home, huddled in front of their black-and-white televisions as they eat supper.

Being stranded on the open prairie, Angela can see why the streets are laid on a grid, man's futile attempt to place a rational structure on the vast, primeval land, which doesn't give a damn if Angela freezes to death in the coming night.

On the corner across from the railway platform, the broken Esso sign clanks in the wind against the metal post. Somewhere a dog barks as the train heads into the distant hills against the burning sky.

Whatever possessed her to come to this desolate place in the middle of nowhere. To get away from her mother. If only.

At times, her mother is frustrating. Like yesterday, her mother, after shopping at the Five&Dime Store, wanted to stop in at an A&W so she could get a bite to eat when Angela wanted to get back home. Her mother went on and on about it, so Angela, relenting, pulled into the A&W parking lot on the next block. But her mother didn't want to go to that A&W, she wanted to go to her regular A&W half-way across the city on North Albert. Christ.

Why do you have to swear after all I'm going through?

The doctor says you don't have cancer.

What do doctors know?

Angela is getting cold. So, as Mr Cox isn't coming, she picks up her suitcase as she will have to find herself a room for the night. She crosses the street to the shabby hotel on the corner across from the Esso. She circles the rusted-out ford truck angle-parked in front of the beer parlour door and goes to the lobby door. She enters the half-dark lobby, which is curtained off from the light coming from the living quarters. Angela rings the bell on the hotel desk. Waits. The sour smell of sauerkraut from the living quarters seeps into the lobby.

Finally, a large, big-hipped woman lumbers through the curtained-off doorway. She pulls the overhead string to the electric light bulb on the tiled ceiling above the hotel desk. Angela asks for a room for the night.

I'll have to ask my husband if he has a room. The woman retreats behind the curtained-off doorway.

On the lobby wall is a reproduction of a purple-mountain landscape. As if prairie people have to fill in the emptiness of the prairie with a background of mountains.

The hotel owner, in an off-white t-shirt, chewing on a toothpick, enters from behind the curtained-off doorway. His big hairy belly is exposed under The T-shirt. He squeezes in behind the hotel desk. I don't have a room for you, he says. Road crew's got the rooms taken up. He rolls up a newspaper and swats a housefly on top of the hotel desk. He scrapes the fly off onto the floor. Maybe you might wanna come back tomorrow when they go home for the weekend.

Angela swallows her desperation. Do you know of a place I could stay the night?

You might try Mrs Briggs down the block, turn right. A block over on the corner is a big brick house.

Long, snotty, black hairs poking out from his large nostrils grosses her out. The slob doesn't give a shit how he looks to people. Probably likes to gross out people.

Is there a place where I could eat?

He spits out his toothpick, missing the garbage pail behind the hotel desk. The chinaman down the street should still be open.

Angela lugs her suitcase back onto the broken sidewalk. The light from the streetlamp on the Esso corner is being swallowed up by the growing darkness of the night. She doesn't belong here. But then she's never belonged. Not even in her own family. Her younger sister, Christine, is the favourite. Angela doesn't measure up to what her mother wants. With her mousy reddish hair and what her mother calls big nose, she isn't pretty like her blonde-haired, blue-eyed sister, who's popular at school. Angela is an outsider, a loner, which is okay with her, because she has her drawing and writing to keep her from going insane.

A black beast of a dog with a massive head like a bear emerges from the dead grass behind the Esso. The beast trots onto the street, stops. Angela, fixed in the beast's gaze, is flooded with fear. But the bitch trots to the telephone pole on the hotel corner and squats in the grass and pisses. Then she disappears behind the side of the hotel.

An old Fargo truck, like her grandfather drove, rattles to a stop in front of the hotel. An older, grey-haired man, dressed in farmer overalls, gets out. You must be the new teacher.

Yes, I'm Angela Kovak. Angela wants to hug him. You don't know how glad I am to see you.

I was starting to think, he says, I was never going to get out of the municipal meeting. Some people never know when to stop talking. Think problems will go away if they keep going on about it. We all are suffering from the drought.

He lifts her suitcase into the back of the truck. We're gonna be in hot water with Mrs. Biggs. She was expecting us an hour ago. Supper's at six. So I guess you've missed supper.

Do you think we could stop at the Chinese cafe . and I could get a soup or something.

Jump in, he says as he climbs up into the cab behind the wheel. Angela steps on the running board and climbs up onto the passenger seat. The hot air blowing from the heater is welcomed.

Here's what we will do, he says. We'll drop your things off at the Brigg's. You can dump off your stuff. Then I'll bring you back to the cafe . You can grab a quick bite while I talk to Benson about how he's making out fixing my tractor. He glances at Angela with those Peter O-'Toole eyes, a handsome face lined by the sun and wind.

Then we'll head over to the school, he says. The principal, Mr Petry, is expecting to see you to give you your timetable for classes tomorrow. Hope you're ready to plunge right in.

I came here to teach, Angela says.

Good to hear, he says as he grinds the gear into reverse and backs into the street. He turns right onto Railway Avenue and heads east where the end of the street empties into the vastness of the prairie. Angela looks up at the gypsy moon.

She feels she can relax as she's in good hands. There's no bad faith in the man. He doesn't know how to be what he isn't. Probably never got to university so he hasn't been told that God is dead.

He is saying that he and the wife will have to have Angela out to the farm for supper sometime. They have a daughter, Fiona, maybe a bit older. Like you, he says, she has a high IQ. I don't know why I'm telling you this.

He turns right onto a side street. He parks in front of a row of overgrown caraganas, gets out and lifts her suitcase from the back of the truck. Angela follows him through the picket fence to the porch. A small, coiffured, grey-haired woman answers the door. I expected you an hour ago, she says sharply.

Mr Cox apologizes for being late. You know how those meetings go. There's always someone who wants to hear himself talk.

You're here now, the matron says.

Mr Cox introduces Angela. As you know, she's taking over for Mr Hancock.

No discipline in that school, Mrs Briggs says. It's no wonder he had a nervous breakdown. Come. I'll show you your room. She heaves herself up the staircase, opens the first door to the right. This will be your room.

The room is small, claustrophobic, a double bed under the slanted ceiling, old style dresser and a small curtained off closet where Angela can hang her clothes. She's told that the bathroom is at the end of the hall.

Mr Cox sets the suitcase on the bedspread. He thanks Mrs. Biggs for taking Angela in.

You look like a nice young lady, Mrs Briggs says. I'm sure we're going to get along just fine. Too bad about Mr Hancock. Back to England, I'm afraid. Not cut out to live out here in the colonies. I do have to say that there's a girl in town. Her name is Simone. Don't let her get close to you. She's evil. Like her mother.

Mr Cox says they should be going. Mr Petry is expecting them at the school.

The man shouldn't be principal, Mrs. Briggs says. Lets the kids run wild. No discipline. It's the parents. They don't teach their children to respect their elders, take responsibility for their actions.

Angela follows the two of them back down the stairs Mrs Briggs tells Mr Cox that she needs him to look at her kitchen window. It's leaking. You can see the windowsill is full of mould.

Angela escapes into the street where she can breathe. It is dark now with a canopy of stars scattered in the night sky.

Mr Cox comes out from the house. He will give her a ride to the chinaman's cafe . Then he'll come back for her, say in half-an-hour.

They get into the truck and Mr Cox backs out and turns right at the corner, down Second Avenue several blocks to Main Street.

I wouldn't wanna be a teacher, Mr Cox is saying. The way kids talk back nowadays. I don't blame Mr Hancock. All he wanted is for his class to go to the school library and pick out something to read. They went to the chinaman's cafe . From what I heard, he told them they could go to hell and walked out. Kids think they can do what they want. There's no consequences. It was worse last year. The French teacher kept a record of students he knew had come to school but skipped his class. He had reams of foolscap of names and dates. He walked out so that something would be done. None of the other teachers supported him. Scared of losing their jobs. So he had no choice but to come back to school. At the end of the year though, the board had to fire the principal when it came out that he had knocked up a grade ten girl.

He parks in front of the cafe . Angela gets down from the truck and goes into the cafe . She is starved. But she won't get a cheque from the school board until next month, so she has to watch her money. Like she can't run out of cigarettes. So she orders soup and coffee.

A plumb waitress brings Angela a coffee. Angela orders lentil soup special. As the waitress takes her order to the kitchen, Angela opens the newspaper left on the table. In Birmingham, Alabama, Martin Luther King is arrested for leading an anti-racist march.

The waitress brings Angela her lentil soup. The name tag pinned on the waitress' uniform says Dory.

I don't get much time to read, Dory says. Not with the two boys. Three. Counting her husband, Larry. She laughs. Don't get me wrong. I'm not complaining. I thank my lucky stars for Larry. He's a good man. A good man is hard to find.

I'm not looking for a man, Angela says.

You're from the city, am I right? Me and Larry lived in the city for a bit. Didn't like it. Too many people. Strangers. Don't know about strangers. What they're up to. Teenyboppers in mini-skirts hanging out on street corners. Winos slobbering on park benches. Business suits strutting their stuff. We came home where we're part of a community. Where people look after each other. Not like in the city where everybody's out for themselves. You should meet my little brother, Leo. He's not little. He's six-four. A real sweetie though. Not married. Beverly broke up with him. I never liked her. Bossed Leo around. He did everything for her. Go buy her cigarettes while she did her nails. I've never blamed him for hitting on Beverly's younger sister. Forget her name. Nancy, I think. Nancy told Beverly. Beverly told Leo she was breaking up with Leo.

I can tell you though, Leo's better off without her. Beverly, I mean. The way she spent his money. Nothing is going to stop her from getting what she wanted. Leo's up to his eye balls in debt. The bugger's still in love with her. Can you believe that? He won't leave the house. Drinking himself silly.

She goes to the kitchen.

Angela opens Sheila Watson's novel, The Double Hook. She loves the starkness of the language, characters cut off from society. Greta at the stove. Turning hotcakes. Reaching for the coffee beans. Grinding away James's voice.

Dory returns. Can I get you anything else?

No, Angela says. Thank you.

Everything okay?

Yes, thank you.

Angela gets up and goes to the washroom to get rid of Dory. She doesn't want to hear about Leo and his problems. She's done with trying to fix other people's problems. She can't. They have to. Like with her mother. But she won't. Her anxieties make her controlling. Did you unplug your bedroom lamp?

Angela goes back to her table. Outside the street window, Cox is angle-parked, waiting for her. Angela pays for her soup and coffee.

You'll have to meet Cox's wife, Dory says. The woman's a piece of work, believe me. Thinks she's so much better than the rest of us. Far as she's concerned, we're white trash.

Angela goes out and gets into the truck.

At the school, she follows Mr Cox to the principal's office where he introduces her to Mr Petry, a small man, bald, with a pasty, round rubber-doll face.

I've been expecting you, Mr Petry says.

Angela Kozak, Angela says.

Yes, yes, he says, getting up from behind his desk and shaking her hand, limply. He sees that Angela is looking at his bedroom slippers. He explains he and his family live just across the street.

He shuffles out of the office into the hallway to show Angela her classroom down from the entrance and washrooms. Your classroom is the last door to the left. You get the morning sun, he says.

Angela and Mr Cox follow Mr Petry to her classroom where he switches on the fluorescent lights. Her six-day rotation is squared off in a pot-potpourri of coloured chalk, red for literature, blue, composition and green for art. Four classes in the morning, as you can see, Mr Petry says, four in the afternoon. The students stay in their rooms while the teachers move from classroom to classroom. That way we're not herding the little beasties back into their next classroom.

I see on the schedule, Mr Petry says, your first class in the morning is literature with the grade twelve. Hamlet, I believe. To be or not to be—that is the question. Yes, well. I will popping in your classes to see how you're doing, he says. I'm a great believer in discipline.

The building itself isn't that old, Mr Cox says. Been what? Nine-ten years?

Opened in nineteen fifty-one, I believe, Mr Petry says. He asks if Angela has any questions.

No, I don't think so.

I hope you're not one of those communist rabble-rousers like we had last year, a Mr Haines, telling his social studies students they should resist authority. They're to do what is right for them.

I'm not anything, Angela says.

Good, I'll lock up and run, Mr Petry says. Time to put the rugrats to bed. His wife is not well. Migraines. Her mother was a stay-at-home mom while her father, a railroad man, worked hard on the job. Hard work doesn't hurt anyone. Self-discipline, that's the ticket. If you want to get ahead in life. It's what's missing nowadays with wanting instant gratification. Everything's instant. Instant coffee. Turn on the TV. Instant shows. Do your own thing. What if everybody did their own thing? Nothing would get done. There would be no houses built. No electricity. No television.

I should be getting Miss Kozak back to her lodgings, Mr Cox says. Been a long day for her.

Long day for all of us, Mr Petrey says.

Angela leaves with Mr Cox who drops her off at the boarding house. In her upstairs cubbyhole, Angela unpacks. What has she got herself into? The principal's a dimwitted moron. Not one original thought in his head. Just a stream of inanities. Like Camus said, stupidity has a way of getting its way. Christ. How do these stupid, self-righteous morons get into positions of power?

She can't do this, she has to. She can't go back home a failure. Be just like you, Angela, her mother would say. How did I give a birth to such a failure. Why can't you be like your sister?

Angela undresses. She is getting fat. Her legs are too short.

In her housecoat, she tiptoes to the bathroom down the hall and runs the water for a hot bath. It wouldn't be asking too much, would it? There is a crack in the ceiling plaster. An Amazon river. Heart of darkness. Dark. Primal. The serpent to be feared, repressed. That part of her. The whore.

Angela soaps her breasts. They are small, perky breasts. It is Christine, who has beautiful full breasts. She is gorgeous. Blonde. Men are attracted to her. Doesn't bother her that she swallows them whole and then spits them out. Ask her boyfriend, Eddie. He knows she's running around on him. But he knows that after her affairs turn to crap, like she's had enough of having to salve their bruised egos, he comes back to her. She tells him men are pricks. But they have pricks. Which is what she wants from men. The orgasms. The path to liberation. She doesn't give a crap what other people think.

Angela should've gone in hairdressing and been her own boss like Christine who doesn't have to worry about being called to the principal's office because, in the Co-op buying socks, she didn't smile at some busybody. Like really.

Angela shampoos her burnt reddish hair. She should cut it short. Be done with it.

She gets out of the tub, dries herself, puts on pyjamas and crawls into bed, turns out the light. She can't fall asleep. Friggin' insomnia. A lifetime of insomnia.

She must've fallen asleep because when she wakes up in the night she remembers her recurring dream in which she's trying to get back to where she wants to be, but the road is flooded. Another recurring dream is that she's in a hospital. She doesn't want to be in the hospital ward where patients sit silently on their beds, their shaved heads bowed. She leaves. The hospital is attached to the university. She's supposed to write an exam. She can't find the exam room. She finds herself in a department store. She likes the coats. But she has to get to the exam room. She takes an elevator, gets out in a hallway. All the doors are locked. She finds herself in the basement. She has to pee. But the toilets are plugged and the overflowed piss is running over the cement floor. She finds a door and escapes outside. She wakes up, goes and pees. She falls back to sleep, waking up in the morning tired.

2

Angela enters the staff room. Mr Petry comes from his office. He introduces her to Mr Jackson, vice-principal, who teaches math; Mr Hawkins, social studies; Mr Skrorud, grade eleven and twelve chemistry and physics; Mrs. Charles, French and librarian; Mr Stevens, phys ed; Miss Valdenson, home ec. Mr Wills is the school unit music teacher and guidance counsellor. The bell rings. The students are herded into the gym where Mr Petry reads the riot act. It has been brought to his attention that somebody has been scrawling pornography on the toilet wall where there is a crude drawing of a naked woman. He wants to know who's responsible.

Angela tells him pornography is in the eye of the beholder. What he sees as pornography, others will see as art.

A senior female student, in dyed black, blunted hair and black mascara eyes, speaks up. I can assure you, Mr Petry, she says, I mean, given the neanderthal intelligence, this charge being brought against whom we all know to be the perpetrator, is malicious in that he didn't know it is an act of crime against art.

Gerald?

Wasn't me.

Yeah, right, an older dark-haired girl says.

Quiet. Nobody is leaving the gym, says Mr Petry, until I know who is responsible. The recess bell rings and the student body scurries into the hallway and outside. Mr Jackson hoofs her outside to see that nobody has lit up a cigarette.

Angela ducks into the staff room for a cigarette. She is joined by Mr Hawkins. The man sprawls in the armchair under the window, his long legs stretched out into the middle of the room. The black-haired student in the men's trousers and white shirt and tie is our notorious Simone Nickleson, he says in an Englishman accent. You have to watch her. She will try to get under your skin. Undermine you. Thinks she's smarter than you. Too smart for her own good. You get to have her in your grade twelve lit and comp classes. Lucky you.

Angela goes to her grade twelve composition class and faces the straight rows of students. There is order in the world.

She reads the opening stanza of T S Elliot's The Hollow Men:

We are the hollow men
We are the stuffed men
Leaning together
Headpiece filled with straw. Alas!
Our dried voices, when
We whisper together
Are quiet and meaningless
As wind in dry grass
Or rats' feet over broken glass
In our dry cellar

Simone wants to know if Angela would take a look at her poem. It's an anti-protest poem about those American protesters, save living with mommie, playing the victim when they weren't getting shot at. Like they were the big-shot martyrs. She gags.

I'd love to, Angela says. The bell rings. She grabs her satchel and heads into the hall in search of her next class. Grade nine art. At the far end of the hallway. She finds them waiting for her. She wants to know where the art room is? There is no art room, she's told. You have to go get the art cart, which has all the art supplies for art.

You're kidding me, right?

We kid you not. It's locked in the storage room. You will have to get the key from Potato-Head.

Angela goes to the principal's office. She's told by the secretary, Mrs Valord, that Mr Petry isn't in his office.

I need the key to storage room.

Yes, of course, you're the new art teacher, Mrs Valord says. An older woman. A fixture in the school. She opens a cupboard door and takes the storage room key down. Here, she says. Bring it right back when you're through.

Yes, of course, Angela says. She finds the storage room door on the far side of the washroom doors. She unlocks the door. There it is. The Mickey-Mouse cart stuffed with art supplies. She grits her teeth and pushes the cart out into the hallway, locks the storage room door and heads to her class, forgetting to drop off the key with Mrs Valord.

She hands out sheets of paper and crayons to have the class draw a portrait of the person next to them. There were cries that they couldn't draw. But some of the students draw childlike portraits with round, lopsided, green eyes, red mouth, rosy cheeks and a humongous nose, the top of the head decorated curlicue hair. The majority, who no longer considered themselves children, in their attempt at realism, drew rigid, mechanical faces, the child-creativity lost, unfortunately.

Somehow she gets through the day. In the staff room, she slumps into the armchair. Bald-headed Jackson is boiling water on the hotplate to make himself a cup of tea. He wants to know if anyone else would like a cup.

Mrs. Charles says she must get home as her children will be wanting to get into the house. Hawkins says she should get a key cut for them.

Yes, she says. I don't know why I haven't thought of that. She dashes out to her car.

Potato-Head comes inside the doorway and stands, scowling. He wants Angela is his office. Now, he says. He marches back to the principal's office. Angela gets up and follows.

It has come to my attention, he says, that, in your grade twelve composition class, you read a story to the class on illicit sex.

There is no sex in the story, Angela says.

I'm told the two characters are having an affair.

I bet there is gossip in town about the affairs going on, Angela says.

Not in my school, he says. And not in composition. The students are to learn to write and punctuate a sentence.

And what is a sentence?

A sentence has a subject and verb and ends with a period, expressing a complete thought.

And what is a complete thought?

Don't get smart with me, young lady.

I'm not. Can we ever write down a complete thought? It would mean we would have to know everything. But nobody knows everything. Can we know anything? Maybe we have no way of knowing.

I'm sure I don't know what you're talking about.

You haven't read Samuel Beckett.

Why do you have to question everything?

Maybe there's a better way. Like why do we put children in a class by age? Why not by IQ? We wouldn't be holding smart children back. As it is, they're end up bored while waiting for the slower students to catch up. If ever. But then, our job is not to teach students to think for themselves, our job is to give our students the skills to take orders.

So cynical at a young age.

May I go?

Yes, yes. Off you go.

Angela goes to her grade twelve literature class. Simone looks up. Didn't take long for you to be called into the principal's office.

Angela tells the class to turn to the Robert Barr's story, A Case of Fever, page one twenty-six.

Why him when he died in nineteen-eleven. This is nineteen sixty-three. Why aren't we reading Doris Lessing's The Golden Notebook?

I've been told I'm to teach you what's on the curriculum.

You caved, Simone says.

She has to, Patsy says. Or lose her job. And we don't want Ms Kozak losing her job.

What about her principles?

Person still has to eat, Patsy says.

If we lose our principles, Jennifer says, then who are we?

We have to be ourselves, Simone says.

Hitler was being himself, Gerald says.

Hitler was evil, Patsy says

We're all evil.

We're basically good.

Until we're not.

It's because the criminal grew up in poverty.

So the evil murderer is a victim?

We still shouldn't let other people define who we are, Simone says. I'll do what I want, when I want, with whoever I want.

And get pregnant.

The pill is going to change all that, Jennifer says. Women will be free to screw around like men.

But there's a downside to the pill, Emily says. A girl will be pressured to have sex. If she doesn't, she will be ostracized from the clique, told she's sexually repressed like her parents. Like my sister was told when she pushed away the toad of a Toronto poet who thought she should feel special he wanted to go to bed with her. Special? Yeah, right. For his self-gratification. Christ, women will be used. And cast aside like a dirty dish rag when he's tired of her and screws her friend.

What about her? Maybe she wants sex.

No wonder there is epidemic of depression among young women, Patsy says.

You need to get laid, Gerald says.

I'm gonna kill him.

I want to be loved, Jennifer says.

Not all of us are desperate to be loved, Simone says. For me, it's more important that I can be free to be myself. Go after what I want out of life.

And what do you want out of life?

I want to live life and not have to give a shit what other people think. Like with my mother who's obsessed with keeping the house spic'nspan. What kind of life is that?

The bible says we should wait until we are married, Patsy says.

Except there is no god, Simone says.

Listen to what you're all talking about, Kathy says. What if Mr Petry walked in?

If there is no god, then everything is permitted, Patsy says.

Nobody has a right to judge me, Simone says.

Then there can be no justice, Emily says.

We should be allowed to do what we want as long as we're not hurting anyone else, Bartley says.

We can't help hurting people when we buy food harvested by underpaid immigrants or clothes that come from sweatshops, Emily says.

We shouldn't have to pay for those doing their own thing and making bad choices, Simone says. Like dropping out of school and going on welfare.

Angela looks at the desks lined up in rows. There is order in the world.

She hands out mimeograph copies of Chekov's Lady with a Dog. The students tell her that they don't have to read stuff that's not in their textbook.

Read, Angela says. I assume you can read.

Don't assume, says the student spokesman. Her name, on the seating plan, reads Simone. Her voice is deep, throaty, masculine. Her dark eyes, wide, intelligent. She is staring at Angela as if Angela is a co-conspirator against mediocrity and stupidity in society. As if the others in class are ignorant apes. Bubblegum mamas more interested in their backcombed, bee-hived hair and red lipstick. Their skin-creamed photographs squared off in the school yearbook. Sweet, little innocents who spread their panty-hosed legs in the back seat of a car for the price of a drive-in movie and a box of buttered popcorn. These little bimbos who have never heard of Charley Parker. The beats. Angelheaded hipsters. That Ginsberg was howling in the negro streets of America. That Sylvia Plath had committed suicide. That Marilyn Monroe was murdered by the mob. That the Russians put up the Berlin Wall while the Americans were stockpiling nuclear bombs and automatic dishwashers.

You're not saying anything?

Sorry, Angela says, I was thinking.

What were you thinking?

Read.

Gerald can't read, Simone says. He doesn't have a brain. He was born brain dead.

Whadda I gotta have a brain fer? I kin make more money on the oil rigs.

He's right, Simone says. Look at Petry. He got an education. A master's degree. The bird brain gets to run the school for next to nothing.

You shouldn't put down birds, someone says. Laughter.

Angela stands at the windows looks out over the grassland to the distant horizon. She turns back to the class. You can learn a lot about writing a short story from Chekov.

Simone says it's about illicit sex. You're gonna be in big trouble with Potato-Head.

Lady With a Dog is about honest emotions, written in unpretentious simplicity. Which is what writing is all about. If you're thinking of becoming a writer to expose the truth of what is going on. I want you to write a short story or poem on what it's like to be with someone of the opposite sex.

You want us to write about sex?

No, Simone. About being with a guy. Or a guy being with a girl. How do they see each other. What do they say to each other. What they do together. Be honest. I get some of you to read your work in class.

Simone says Gerald can't read.

And you can't take apart a motor and put it back together.

Wanna bet?

Yeah, right.

I want to know what you think, Angela says.

Nobody ever asks what we think, says Simone. We're told what to think.

I'm here, Angela says, to help you learn how to think for yourselves.

The bell rings. Angela goes to her next class where the grade nines tell her they want to finger paint.

Like in kindergarten?

No. Back then, we were told to not colour over the lines.

From her cart, Angela takes out the paints and paper and empty tuna cans for water containers. I want you to paint masks. For next class, I'm going to bring you pictures of primitive portraits painted by Picasso and later Karl Appel. During the Renaissance, artists painted ideal representations, of what man could be. Later, Goya and Rembrandt painted how they saw man as he was. The Romantics in last century went back to how they wanted man to be. Then modern artists came along and distorted how people looked to show the stress and anxiety of living in the modern world where we're alienated, cut off from the natural world, from ourselves, our spirituality. Who were we in a world without meaning. The universe running by random chance.

Angela stops. By the look on their blank faces, she knows she has lost them. The point I'm trying to make is that everybody wears masks. We get dressed up and make sure we look good in the mirror before we leave the house.

Except for Fat Patty, Bradley says. She never looks good.

That's not very nice, Patty says. You have to apologize.

What's the big deal?

The big deal, Bradley Petry, Angela says, we don't judge people on how they look, we judge them on what they do. You have a big nose, a real honker, what if I didn't call you by your name, but I called you Honker.

I like that. Honker. Honk honk.

Apologize.

I'm sorry, Patty.

No you're not.

Patty?

He's not.

Why are you being mean?

I'm not.

You are.

I'm sorry.

Angela walks up and down the aisles of desks to observe their work.

Mine's a mess, Cindy says.

Life is a mess.

Yuk.

Yeah but I want it to be perfect.

Everything in its place,

Yes.

You want to be obsessive compulsive.

I don't know what that means.

Being rigid.

Bernard created a monstrous mask with eye holes. He puts the mask over his face and, getting up from his desk, pulling one leg behind him, his hands clawing the air in front of the faces of the girls in the classroom. The girls shriek. You're not funny.

My cat died, Frances says.

I'm so sorry, Angela says.

Me too, Frances says.

Jack smears what paint he still has on his fingers on Lucy's painting.

He ruined it, Lucy says.

No, I didn't, he says. I fixed it up.

Angela goes over and stands over him. Who told you to?

I did.

You gave yourself permission?

I guess.

Lucy can then give herself permission to tell you that you're an asshole.

You can't swear like that.

I gave myself permission. Are you going to apologize?

What for?

For ruining Lucy's painting.

It wasn't very good, Jack says.

Who made you the judge?

I did.

I want you to write an apology, which will be tacked on the school bulletin board.

Com'on, Jack says. She's just fat Cherry.

You will write out a second apology for calling her names.

That's who she is.

You are going to stay in your desk until you have written out: I apologize for ruining Lucy's painting and I apologize for calling Lucy names. Each a hundred times.

I have to get home, he says.

Then be quick about it, Angela says, because you're not leaving your desk until you do. Even if it takes you to supper time. And if not today, you will stay in tomorrow and the day after that until you do.

Fuck you, he says.

That's it. Leave my class. Don't come back.

You can't do that.

Wanna bet?

You just have it in for me.

I have it in for bullies.

You're bullying me, Jack says.

Apologize.

No.

Get out.

You can't kick me out?

I just did.

You're gonna hear from my dad.

Is he a bully too?

Jack leaves. The class is silent.

Start cleaning up, Angela says. The bell is going to ring. Angela asks Lucy if she will take the cart of art supplies to the storage room. She can get the key from Mrs Valord.

Angela goes to the staff room. Petry storms in. He wants to talk to Angela in his office.

Angela follows him to the principal's office where she is told she can't kick Jack out of class and not let him back in. Does she not know who his father is? John Weston, who happens to own half-the-town.

He doesn't own me, Angela says.

You know boys-will-be-boys.

They don't have to be bullies.

Ah, here is Mr Weston now. Com'in, Mr Weston. I''m sorry for having to ask for you to come.

You must be Ms Kozak, says Mr Wesley, who doesn't look at all like a George Grosz's caricature of a fat capitalist. Actually, he is rather good-looking with his shaved, chiselled-chin look. Like a Hollywood actor. Probably could've been an actor. Like Christine could've been an actress. She is beautiful enough. Gorgeous figure. Sex-pot. Like Jane Mansfield.

Petry explains how Ms Kozak took it upon herself to kick Jack out of her class.

What did he do?

He defaced Lucy's painting. Refuses to apologize. Then called her names. Then swore at me, Angela says.

Being a little shit, Mr Weston says.

Yes.

She won't let him back into her class.

There are consequences, Mr Wesley says. Where is he now?

He's gone home, I suspect, Angela says.

Thank you, Ms Kozak. We need teachers who aren't afraid to put their foot down. I'm off then.

Angela turns to go.

I've been told you had your student paint grotesque masks to ward off evil spirits like the savages, Petry says, scowling. We don't believe in evil spirits, Ms Kosak. You were scaring your students that there were evil spirits.

He turned the pages of a prairie art book from the library. Folk paintings of wheat fields and grain elevators and clouds floating in the blue sky. Of horses running wild. Paintings of farmers and their wives bent over in the field. Art, according to the gospel of Petry, should be moral, uplifting.

Angela leaves. She goes to the staff room and slumps into the armchair. Boy, I'm glad this day is over. The staff room empties. She pulls out John Newlove's book of poems. Poems of her own place, growing up on the Saskatchewan prairie like driving through the snow a"banked in the moonlight."

Angela butts her cigarette, grabs her purse and coat, heads out onto the prairie. The sun is warm in the silence. The silence stills her. She moves into the silence.

3

Back in her room, Angela sacks out on her bed. She's been told she is not to have her students finger painting grotesque masks like a bunch of heathens. Petry cleared his throat, scowled. You probably think it's modern art. He showed her real art. A painting on his office wall of a farmer and his wife toiling in a field of golden sheaves.

Yeah, right. Clichés of a primitive past, when men were men and women were women, pure, positive thinking Nazis types. Art, according to the gospel of Petry, should be moral, uplifting. It should educate our wards so they would know and be proud of where they came from.

What did she think she was doing reading poetry to the grade elevens? He doesn't want her bringing Ferringetti, or whatever his name is, into the class room. We have modern poets. Archibald Lampman. Bliss Carman. Duncan Campbell Scott.

All born in the nineteenth century, she wants to say. But he is telling her that he wants her to teach the sentence. A sentence begins with a capital and ends with a period. A sentence expresses a complete thought.

What is an incomplete thought? How do we know? Good question. But that's philosophy and she is not to teach philosophy. She is to watch for split infinitives. Police students' spelling. The dictionary meaning of words. All laid out. The answers in the back of the textbook. Nobody has to think. The thinking is done for them. Those in power cannot have the masses thinking for themselves. They have to be told what to think, what they can say, believe. It's called propaganda. There is no god. Make up your own right and wrong. Conservatives are fascists.

Petry's saying that he's been watching her through the class door window. She has rapport, he said, sure that she was going to fit in nicely. You potential to be an excellent teacher.

Angela thanked him. Excused herself. She went to the storage closet to get her art supplies on the mickey mouse cart she pushed from class to class. She shut the door and slid to the floor. She couldn't stop the hot tears from scalding her makeup. She stopped crying and wiped her eyes, blew her nose in the kleenix. Don't let the bastards get her down.

She puts on her coat and descends to the outside door and enters the coming night where she walks to the edge of town onto the prairie where the sky smoulders on the distant hill. The open space, the silence, regenerates her soul.

The next day, Angela tells her grade twelve class that she has asked the public librarian downtown to bring in copies of the book, To Kill A Mockingbird in which a black, who is charged with the rape of a white girl, is defended by a white lawyer. The novel exposes the evils of racism in the American south.

Nothing to do with us, Gerald says.

When we segregate Indians on reservations, Jennifer says.

They agreed to go on reserves when they signed them treaties, Gerald says.

4

Sunday. The house is empty, silent. Mrs Briggs must've gone to church. Angela has nothing against the church. She doesn't go herself. Not anymore. Not after. She doesn't want to think about it.

The hot tears scald her eyes. She isn't going to cry. She is finished with crying. She isn't finished. It will never be finished. The lump inside her. Like a cancerous growth. Pulling her down. She can't let it pull her down. The feeling she is dead.

She lights a cigarette. She shouldn't smoke. It's a death wish.

She pours herself a drink. Another drink. Another. Drinking herself into a stupor. She passes out and when she wakes up, it starts all over. Over and over and over.

Maybe she should have had him charged. Even though he'd get off, he'd still have the stigma of being accused of being a rapist. But then everybody would know she was raped. She's stuck with the humiliation, the violation.

She looks at herself in the mirror. She's a wreck. A shell of the person she was.

Hot tears scald her eyes. Damn him. She has her teaching degree, life should be good, she's independent. She can teach to make a living so she can paint and write. But he ripped the joive de vie out of her. Her life aborted.

Angela escapes into the street. The warm sun melts the frozen ruts in the street. The smell of mud. Earth. A crow calls from the poplar trees across the railway tracks. An old man in his eighties is digging trenches for the water to run off his yard. He shoos the cat from the branches in the warted elm tree. The cat skirts up the drainage pipe down the corner of the house. The old man goes back to his digging.

Angela heads for Main Street. The side streets are deserted. Like the town people are on hold, waiting for something to happen in their lives. She turns back. On the front steps of the house, she lights a cigarette. God help us when a mediocre little man gets to play principal in his prison-block school where the inmates have no real connection to the outside world. They're locked up in a world where things are done like they've always been done. It's written down in the curriculum. And when the inmates are finished the girls will be women. They will marry one of the guys and have children while he ends up working for the local lumber yard or driving the Co-op fuel truck. Some will farm with their fathers. Few will get away. Simone, Emily, may escape and go to university.

Angela has to get away. Take on the outside world. She finishes her cigarette and turns back toward the house. She goes in and ventures into the spic'nspan kitchen. The woman is anal retentive. Poor Joe. The man must've never got laid. He might spill his semen and she just put clean sheets on the bed.

Angela makes herself a cup of instant coffee and goes back up to her room to wait for dinner. She lights a cigarette. She should write some letters. Let people know she's all right. She's not all right. The sick howling of the hound across the back alley all hours of the night is ruining her sleep.

Next door to the Brigg's house live an older couple, retired. Mrs. Biggs says, for years, he was a Watkins man. She bought her cold remedies and puddings from him. The man liked to talk. Talk, talk, talk. If it wasn't the weather, it was his aches and pains. His false teeth not fitting. She couldn't get him out of the house.

Angela wanders around the living room looking at the family photographs framed on the doily-covered shelves on the walls and the dining table. There is a photo of an older man in white shirt and tie. He is wearing his Sunday hat. A sadness in his eyes. The matron's late husband. She had said his name was Joe. He had worked for the town. A good man. Salt of the earth. Never complained. Even at the last. On his deathbed, he told her she should remarry. He didn't want her to be alone in the big house.

The two children in the photographs must be Beth and Robert. There is a coloured picture of Beth in her pink, crinoline graduation dress and white gloves and white high-heels, her hair piled in a beehive. She is married with two children, Amanda and Curtis. The girl is a quiet one, with thick glasses, always reading a book. Curtis is a going concern, into everything. Beth can't keep up. If he's not unrolling toilet paper through the house, he's climbing into the cupboards pulling out all her pots and pans. He's going to be the death of the woman. Bob isn't much help with the children. He feeds them ice cream and pop. The man's an accountant with the bank in Swift Current. Mrs. Briggs never sees the grandchildren. Bob and Beth are so busy with their lives. Beth has her garden. Mrs. Briggs can't garden anymore. It's the arthritis in her hands. And she's getting old, forgetful. She can't remember where she puts things. Beth says she is repeating herself. Angela picks up the photograph of Byron in his sailor uniform on board the HMS Elizabeth. He got away from this place.

In the late afternoon, the sky is clouded over. Before it rains. Angela puts on her coat and walks to the edge of town. She crosses through the ditch to the railway tracks and heads into the prairie, which is full of debilitated barns and abandoned churches. A way of life when everybody looked after each other. No television, everybody came and visited, sitting at the kitchen table under a kerosene lamp telling stories.

Angela is liking the open prairie where she could walk forever and never get to the horizon. Nothing but the land and the sky and the silence. She drawn into the silence, the spirits of the Indian tribes who lived here on the prairies for thousands of years. By the spirits. They are lonely and want her to come away with them. She is tempted. Yes. Go with them and leave everything behind. To forget.

She turns back. How easily a person could lose herself. Lose her direction. The silence is too much. She is thinking too much. Her thoughts racing. Petry. Briggs. Wanting to run her life for her. Make her into their image. Not after what happened. Not after what he made her. A whore.

Maybe she should write poetry. Dig into the unconscious to work out the ugly feelings she is made to live with.

Maybe from her dark side, she had wanted to be a whore and he tore off her veil. No. He has a name. Damien. He raped her. Made her into his image. A whore who wanted it. Goddamn him.

She has to get outta here. Back into anonymity to the city where she can lose herself. Get back to being herself. Away from prying eyes that can see right through her.

She has to stop the self-pity. Not good. A disease.

Write. Paint. Help her understand what the rape did to her. So bloody naive going with him to his studio. The fucking rage inside her. The injustice.

She climbs down off the railway tracks into the stubblefield. The prairie soothes her. It's there for her. Eternally there.

She hates having no money. Person can't even go for a cup of coffee. All her life. Being poor. Going without. Living in that small house on the north end. Her father a sewing machine salesman. An alcoholic. Her mother knew when she married him that he drank. But she could fix him, get him off the booze. He's a good man when he isn't drinking. But he drinks up what little money there is. She can't leave him, he needs her. To make ends meet, she works in the Empire Hotel restaurant where she's on her feet all day, comes home, cooks supper, cleans up the kitchen, takes out the garbage. Before bed, she puts rollers in her hair. Screams at the girls if they're late coming home at night.

Somehow Angela falls asleep. She dreams she's to write an exam but she can't find the room. She is in a department store where she can't find the shoes she wants. She takes the elevator and gets out on a hospital floor. The rooms are full of patients who sit on their beds, staring at her like she's crazy. The nurses won't stop in the hallways to tell her how to get out. She finds herself in the basement. She has to pee. But the toilets are plugged and the water is running over the concrete floor. She finds some stairs and escapes outside where there is a playground with swings and teeter-totters. She heads across the playground into the labyrinth of dark streets.

5

Angela sits in the principal's office. Look at him. Petry with his round, rubberdoll face. Angela wants to poke his rubberdoll face with her finger. See if the face would pop back out.

The man is making her wait while he pretends to clear some papers off his desk. He is a busy man. Doesn't she know that?

He looks up. His bottom lip is curled into a scowl. Doesn't even know how ridiculous he looks. Angela wants to laugh. She doesn't. She lights a cigarette while Mr. Petry drones on about the great responsibilities teachers have to their students. Teachers are to set an example. The students are tomorrow's citizens. Teachers are the potters, students are the clay. It is her job to mould her students into responsible (obedient) citizens who will do what they're told. A teacher has to be on top of things. Know everything. And here he is. This stupid, rubber-doll-face, inane man spouting non sequiturs. And he will still be here in his little principal's office running things long after she has been fired for not following his rules.

You know why you're here.

Not really.

He looks up at her, clears his throat, scowls. Please put out your cigarette. Why do you have to smoke? Makes you look cheap, like a cheap whore on the corner under a streetlamp. Not a good role model for your students.

I'm not a whore.

I'm not saying you are.

But I look like a cheap whore.

No, no, no, you misunderstand me. I'm talking about being a role model students can look up to.

I think you're hoping I'm a cheap whore. I'd let you bend me over your desk and you'd pull up my skirt and...

No no no. You misunderstand me. I wasn't thinking anything of the kind.

But you've thought about it.

Angela gets to the feet and exits the principal's office. How did she end up with this inane little man being her principal. He'd never talk to Hawkins like that.

She goes back to class. It's Friday. After classes, Angela stops in the Princess Hotel and treats herself to a cold beer.

You're the new teacher, the barmaid says. You could be fired if the school board hears you came in and had a beer.

What? Because I'm female? But the male teachers can come and drink all the beer they want? It's bullshit.

What we women have to put up with?

Angela lights a cigarette and tries reading her paperback. She can't help but overhear the conversation a few tables down where a young couple are in the midst of an argument. The young man in the blond brush cut wants to know when he is going to see her again. She doesn't know. I'll have to think about it, she says, a pretty brunette in a high school jacket from a few years ago.

Angela looks down at the page of her paperback. She shouldn't be listening. She pretends to read, listening. The young woman is saying she needs space. It's getting too serious.

But I love you, he says.

Don't say that.

You don't want to be loved.

No. It scares me, she says. Love can be so easily taken away.

I'm not George Helman.

I know. But I can't do this.

I'll always love you.

Then I 'm sorry for you. She gets up, zips up her jacket, picks up her purse.

This is it then?

Yes, she says and heads for the street door. He turns and looks out the street window to hide the tears. Poor sod.

Angela turns back to her paperback. The big woman at the next table says Angela must be the new teacher. I should've bin a teacher, she says, laughing through bad teeth. Get to sit on my ass all day and get paid for it.

There is no help for stupid people. They will always be among us.

She is joined by Mr. Wills. May I join you?

Yes, of course. How are you?

The bartender says he doesn't serve faggots. His crony grins to himself. He knows he's not a faggot. He's a real man like the bartender. Maybe your girlfriend there, the hotel owner says to Mr. Wills, would like a real man. Make a woman out of her. The crony chuckles.

I'm not asking for trouble, says Mr. Wills. The bartender comes from behind the bar. Maybe you want I show you the door.

I'm sure that's not necessary, says Mr. Wills. He backs to the door and slips out into the dark street.

Stupid faggot, says the crony. Makes a man sick.

Want another beer?

Angela says she has to go. She gathers her things and leaves. She has to get out of this place. Maybe the west coast. Vancouver. So expensive out there.

Angela goes to the cafe for a plate of french fries and gravy. Dotty's in good spirits. Her usual chipper self. Larry's got a new job driving the truck for Liberty

Transport. He will be gone most of the time, sometimes as far as Montreal, can you believe it?

She's never been anywhere herself. Once. The family drove to Ontario. Her grandmother's sister. Flo. She was born in Ontario. Their mother didn't want to bring a baby out west. Flo was left with family in Ontario. The two sisters grew up separate. Grandma here in Saskatchewan. Flo in Ontario. They wrote each other but it was years, grandma maybe in her fifties, before she got to take the train to see her sister, Flo.

Flo had grown up on the farm in Ontario where she did all the chores, milking cows, gathering eggs, the garden, while her aunt sat by the stove and drank tea. Flo never married.

Person never knows the half-of-it, Dotty says. The stories about what went on behind closed doors. Like the old woman across the back alley from the Briggs's house. The little yellow house. Her name is Aurea. She is the oldest of seven girls. All of them, except her, have moved away or died.

Back when they were kids, their father left the farm and went to sign up for the war. The army sent him back home, he was sterile. Dotty laughs. So who were the fathers? Probably them that came out in the dirty thirties looking for work on the threshing crews.

You've heard the story about Mrs. Briggs's father and his twin brother. They were identical. Their wives couldn't tell them apart. So the two of them would sleep with each other's wife. Until the women made one of them grow a moustache so they could tell who was who. The buggers.

Few years back, there was a teacher, a Mrs Ducet, with her son, Alain, a good-looking kid. Played hockey. From what I heard, she let him sleep with her. You can imagine what went on. A horny teenager in bed with a grown woman. People, heh?

Simone went out with him. He wanted her to tell him she loved him. She said she didn't. He said he was going to kill himself. She said to go ahead if that was what he wanted. His mother found him hanging from the rafters in the house.

You've heard about Fenton Cox. The guy thought he was really something the way he drove around in his red convertible. People don't talk about it but he knocked up the Kubick girl. Her father was bought off. Fenton's mother saw to that. She wasn't having her little boy marrying a little immigrant tramp from the wrong side of the tracks. The whole lot of them should be sent back to where they came from. Bad enough the Jews own half-the-town.

The way the woman comes in here in her fur coat, her nose stuck up in the air. Person would think she was royalty the way people bow down to her, Dotty says.

Angela walks along Railway Avenue which empties onto the grid road which runs east to the horizon. The clouds are a deep purple as the sun starts to set. She wraps herself in the blanket against the cold wind coming off the hills behind her. She tries not to think. Clear her head of thoughts. Cleansing herself. Baptismal. Of sorts.

She goes up to her room and undresses, puts on her housecoat and goes to the upstairs bathroom where she takes a long hot bath to warm up. She should wash her hair. Maybe not.

Back in her room, she stays in her housecoat. But her room is small, suffocating. She crawls into bed, and in the warmth of the bed, falls asleep. She dreams about snakes. They're in her bedroom. She is afraid. Wakes up. She has a hard time going back to sleep.

6

Saturday. Angela stays in bed. Mrs Briggs walks into her room. She wants to know if Angela is sick. You didn't come down for breakfast.

Angela says she's not hungry. She's very tired.

You should eat something.

Angela says she will. Right now, she wants to sleep. She didn't sleep last night.

Mrs Briggs says it is being in a strange place.

Yes, Angela says.

Mrs Briggs lumbers back down the stairs. Angela reads. She falls asleep. It is dark when she wakes up. She's missed supper. She doesn't have the money to go to the cafe .

The woman from the photographs, Beth, with her big, wide eyes and bucktooth smile, comes into Angela's room. She puts a vodka on the night table, pours two shot glasses. Thought you probably needed shot.

Angela downs her shot. You must be Beth.

What's mother been saying about me?

You're married, two children, the quiet-one Amanda and the going concern two-year old, Curtis.

If I'm not watching, Beth says, Curtis is wrapping the trees with toilet paper or climbing into the cupboards pulling out all my pots and pans. He's going to be the death of me. Ricardo isn't much help with the children. He feeds them ice cream and Pepsi. He's an accountant with the bank in Swift Current. Mom's upset we had to move so far away, she never gets to see the grandchildren.

And your brother Byron in the photograph?

He joined the Navy to get away.

Your late dad looks so sad in the photographs.

Beth pours them another shot. They both down the shots.

I've heard a lot about you, Beth says. You've made quite a hit with the kids at school. You don't just lecture, you listen to them. Let them say what they think.

I learn a lot from them.

I should introduce you to Henry Miner, Beth says. I almost married him myself. He's taken over his dad's big farm. He's got money and nobody to spend it on.

So why didn't you marry him?

And be tied down in this shithole of a town, no thanks, Beth says.

But it would be okay for me, Angela says.

You don't know it's a shithole yet.

I'm learning, Angela says.

I should have stayed though and married Henry, but no, Beth says, I had to chase after Ricardo. In high school, he was cool. In the big world out there, which I learned after I married him, he was just another guy. Nobody thought he was cool. He struggled to keep a job. In the end, he gave up and drank. He's on the streets of Edmonton somewhere. I've lost track of him.

You should come home and marry Henry, Angela says.

Maybe I should. He is a good man. Quiet. Bit overweight. But not bad looking. I could nurse over in Mansfield. Have you ever run into a Vivian, my best friend back in the day. She married Mark Horn when she should've gone to university. In school, she was brilliant. Won all the awards in grade twelve. No, no. She stayed and had five children. What a waste. I hear she keeps books for Cox Motors in town. Her sister, Harriet, married a farmer across the river. They have a few cattle. To make a go of it, he's gone most of the time, a roughneck on the oil rigs. A man shouldn't leave his wife alone. There's talk that Darren, who lives with parents on their farm along the river, has been seen crossing the hills on horseback just as the sun comes up, coming from the direction of Harriet's place.

My mother will be wondering where I got to. You want children?

Not really, Angela says.

You have somebody?

No, Angela says.

You're going to have to meet our Byron. Though we never see much of him. He took a degree in engineering. He's now saving the world in Africa building safe water plants.

Beth stretches out her legs, her feet raised off the floor. Do you think I have nice ankles? I think I have thick ankles. Vivian doesn't have thick ankles. She is born perfect. Do I sound envious? I'm not, she says. I like my life. Most of the time. How about you? Do you like it here?

I like being out on the prairie, Angela says. It has soul. Like an old woman who's been there like forever.

7

Hawkins comes into the cafe and joins Angela at her table. He bums a cigarette. Thought you quit smoking, Angela says.

I did, he says. He lights the cigarette. Exhales. You'll never learn, will you. You think your job is to educate these kids. The pursuit of knowledge. Truth. Except there is no truth. Except what people make up. No intelligence needed. What they feel. You could be feeling I'm a dirty old man wanting to get you into bed.

Are you?

What man isn't? You're young, you've got intelligent eyes, a great body.

Yeah, right.

I can never understand why attractive women don't see it themselves?

Too critical.

Change what you can. Then let it go. I could get rid of the beer belly. But I'd have to exercise. And I don't. So I live with it. It's like reading the newspaper. All the shit and corruption going on. But what can I do about it? I'm too old to go over fight in their wars.

He sounds like an old and tired out man, his shoulders hunched over in defeat.

I've been told you lost a son sliding on the ice under a semi.

I don't think the wife is ever going to recover.

I'm so sorry.

Nobody promised us a rose garden.

How did you end up in the boondocks?

I needed a job. I had applied to social services in Calgary. But, in the evening, I'd accepted this teaching job. I got a call the next morning from Calgary.

You could've raised your children in Calgary.

Accepting on the phone put me under contract to come here.

But you've stayed here in the middle of nowhere.

I'm not out to change the world, Hawkins says.

The path of least resistance.

Hawkins laughs. Human nature.

Ergo, the status quo.

Run like hell because those who want change want to change you, Hawkins says.

You're okay with the grinding poverty on our Indian reservations?

I didn't put them there.

Don't you have any compassion?

Not up to me to make life better for them. It's up to them. But their tribal culture doesn't allow them to get ahead. Like in the tribe, it's custom to allow others to borrow your axe to chop down trees for firewood. But what if they borrow your Chevy pickup and get into an alture and he tells the story of an Indian starting a pig farm. He got his pig barn burned to the ground.

I don't believe you.

You're free to believe what you want.

Hawkins gets up, pays for his and her coffee and leaves.

A pack of students in their green and gold, high school jackets crowd into the cafe . They grab wet coke bottles from the cooler and commandeer the tables in the back of the cafe where they play the jukebox and gossip. Angela never was part of the high school in-crowd . Never tried to be. She wasn't good at small-talk about makeup and boys and what dorks they are.

Simone comes into the cafe. She has cropped her black hair . Looks good on her. The dark girl.

Simone sits down across from Angela. You free this weekend?

I have papers to mark, Angela says.

The crowd bursts into the street, bellowing like a herd of rhinoceros as they pile into their cars. The cars start up and roar, apocalyptic beasts, backing up into the street. A wave out the window from little boys living dangerously. So scared they're nothing. That they don't measure up. Never will. They will end up driving the town garbage truck, getting old and ending up slobbering into their soup. For now, they strut. Cockadoodledoo.

The night has turned cold, Simone says. She looks at Angela, into her eyes, her own eyes unblinking, cat-like. Angela becomes self-conscious. Like Simone can see inside her. She knows. Knows everything. Angela can sense it. A mean-streak in her. The way she delights in putting down her inferiors.

Simone turns up the collar on her black leather jacket. She looks down on Angela from her height. Want a ride?

Thanks, but I'd like to walk. I need the air.

Suit yourself. Simone goes back to her black Chevy Nova SS and climbs in behind the steering wheel. She backs into the street and takes off, spitting up the gravel.

Angela looks up at the stars in the cold, indifferent universe.

She trusted him. He was a friend. Wanting to believe people are basically good. They're not. Men think they have a right to take what they want.

Christine is okay giving them what they want. They make her feel attractive. She should be with all the money she spends on makeup and clothes. But, after she's finished painting her eyelids, putting on her false eyelashes, mascara, she doesn't look like Christine. She looks like a party doll, a show girl ready for a performance, the shooting of a movie for which she is scriptwriter-producer-director, giving herself the biggest part. The rest of her family and friends get bit parts. They don't play their parts how she wants, they end up on the editing floor. The world could be on the brink of a nuclear war, Christine is going to go shopping. She can't afford it. But she saw the most gorgeous, little dress in Shirley's. Two of them in fact. Angela has to help her decide.

Angela can't be what she isn't. It's not authentic. She's not like her sister. Christine is tall and beautiful. Angela has short legs and wide hips like her mother. Christine takes after their father. Christine is his favourite. With him, she can still get a way with blue murder.

Growing up, Angela was the scapegoat in the family. She got blamed for the mess in the house. It was her job to wash the dishes, the floors, take the garbage out. Christine got to bake cakes.

And Simone, she is being nice because she wants to know all about me, how many men I've slept with, my secret affairs with married men. She herself is having a secret affair with the young lawyer in town. That he is married means she doesn't have to commit. For her, it's just sex. Sex is sex, right?

Angela can't let anybody get close. Especially Simone. She will see through her, her shame. Her fault she was raped.

Angela has to be careful around Simone, who plays by her own rules. And a person doesn't always know what the rules are.

8

It's after school. Everyone is gone. Angela is alone in the staff room. The leftover coffee is bitter. She should make a fresh cup. What is it with her, she can't go along with what's she told? Why does she have to challenge everything? Why can't she be more compromising? The others are quite happy with the way things are. They don't see anything wrong with spoon feeding slop to the students. Maybe they believe in the slop. Two plus two equals four. Four legs good, two legs better. Stop thinking, stop thinking, stop thinking. What good is thinking? It goes around and around, never gets anywhere, except to wear her down.

The next day in her grade twelve class, she dumps all the textbooks into the garbage. We're just going to read what we want and talk about what we want, she says.

You'll get fired, Gerald says.

They have to give me notice and by then, it will be the end of the school year. What do you want to talk about?

Sex, Gerald says.

Wonderful stuff, Angela says. Next.

Equal rights for women, Patricia says.

We've had the Bill of Rights in this province since forty-seven, Leo Jenkins says from the back of the room.

Didn't stop women being discriminated against, Patricia says.

Then enforce the Bill of Rights, Harold says.

It's different for women, Patricia says.

Because you say it is, Harold says.

Do you help your mother with the dishes?

Yeah.

Washing and ironing clothes.

That's her job, mine is to take out the garbage and mow the lawn. And, in winter, shovel snow in a country where we have snow seven months of the year.

I have to wash floors, Gerald says.

You wash the floors?

Every Saturday morning because I've come in late. The class laughs.

Patricia's right, Angela says. There's never been a female prime minister.

Because women get themselves pregnant, Simone says. Get stuck at home with dirty diapers and sour pablum.

Before going back to her digs after school, Angela walks out on the prairie. She stays out until it's dark and the full moon is broken up into jewelled shards strewn on the dark waters of the river. The river lisps against the silence of the hills.

Angela listens for the bark of the coyotes.

She returns to the town streets and stops in at the town library. It is a small library where the books smell old and musty. She runs her finger down the spine of the old books. She finds War and Peace. Anna Karenina. Brothers Karamazov. Sons and Fathers. Dead Souls. A retired teacher, Mr Kuziuk donated them, says the librarian. A Ukrainian from the old country.

Angela signs out Anna Karenina. A man in the old suit and boots turns from the book stacks. He has long hair and a grey beard, his eyes laughing at her. You're the new teacher. A real shit-disturber from what I hear.

We need shit-disturbers, the librarian says. She's a small woman in a shawl with short grey hair, bright, intelligent eyes. She lives with her husband brought down by multiple sclerosis. Angela often sees him in his wheelchair, taking in the sun. Says hi.

Angela leaves them to it. She needs a drink. There's still a drop or two left in her rum bottle up in her digs.

9

The next day, in the staff room, Miss Valdenson is showing off her new green and pink spring coat. She is wearing a pink dress and pink stockings with green shoes. The Easter break had been absolutely great. She had driven to Medicine Hat with her girlfriend, Sheila. They had shopped till they dropped. I found a shag lamp for hanging over the chesterfield, she says. Heaven knows she needs more light in the house. It's so dark. Depressing, she says.

Her cat, Miss Mew, says Mrs. Charles, has been depressed.

Petry comes into the staff room. He stands inside the doorway, surveys the room, scowling so everybody will know he is the principal. He doesn't want to be seen to be too chummy with his staff. Yet, the man is desperate to be accepted. Probably like back in school where he was ignored by the other kids.

No one notices him in the doorway except Angela who is sitting facing the doorway. Petry turns on his heels, muttering something about the paperwork piling up on his desk.

Outside the door, in the hallway, he says hello to Mr Jaworski, who grunts back. In his white lab coat, a confirmed bachelor in his fifties, Mr Jaworski is heading to the chem lab where he holes up, arranging and rearranging test tubes and Bunsen burners for class experiments.

Angela pours herself another coffee and waits for the bell.

Back in class, she wants her students to write on what they did over the weekend. Simone says Angela wouldn't want to know.

The bell rings. The students salivate and file out of the classroom. Angela goes to the washroom to pee and get away from everybody.

In her next class, she has her grade nines draw a grid road and telephone poles in perspective against a flat horizon. She slips out the back door for a cigarette. After school, she will dribble the ball with the girls' basketball team. Then she will shower in the school showers and go to the house for supper. She will eat the roast beef, potatoes and gravy and carrots. Then she will go up to her digs, depressed. Not good. She can't let herself go down. It's too hard to get herself back up. She should quit her job. She can't quit. It would be admitting they got to her.

She gets her sketch book and sketches a raw self-portrait. Without thinking. Without looking at the paper. She draws a Richard's nude woman. Thick, heavily lined. Her primeval prairie woman that rises up from the muck. Begotten not made.

She lights a cigarette and looks at her drawing. The power in the heavy black lines. Her power. Rising up in her. Don't let the bastards get you down. You can't be different. A person who doesn't watch TV. She reads books. Thinks she's so much smarter than the rest of them. They don't want people to get ahead. She's to be like them. Their complicity in the status quo. Doing things the way they have always been done. Never evolving. They'd still be washing clothes by hand if Westinghouse hadn't come up their automatic washing machine.

At the post office, she picks up a letter from Jason, who writes he is coming to see her. She hasn't told him she was raped. She writes for him to forget about her.

10

That evening, she walks through the dark streets to the library. The library is quiet. An oasis from the school, the town. Nobody comes to the library. Except for the small woman, with chopped hair and dark eyes, in her forties, pretty once. She sits at a table and reads. She never takes a book home.

Beautiful night, Angela says.

I wish it would warm up, the woman says. She hides the title of the book she is reading. As if she is reading smut.

I'm Angela.

Teresa. You're the new school teacher. So you haven't been her long. You don't know what people are like here. Lies. Even God lied. He's evil. He lets bad things happen.

She closes the book and turns the title to the table. She leaves the library. Angela picks up the book. Stone Angel.

It's several weeks before Angela sees the woman in the library again. Why are you wearing sunglasses?

Don't ask. I have to get home. Leroy will be looking for me.

You can't go back, Angela says.

Where'm I gonna go?

Your parents, Angela says.

Father kicked me out for getting pregnant.

What kind of man is he that he can't see his child needs help?

You don't know him. He talks to father-god all the time.

We have to find you a safe place.

There is no safe place. She leaves the library.

A terrible loneliness comes over Angela. She drags herself up to her room and, in the dark, opens a bottle of wine. A car's headlight through the window crosses the flowered wallpaper. Then it is dark again. Like the woman in library, she feels so alone in the world. Nobody to hold her. To love her. To make her feel that she mattered.

She turns on the light. Looks in the dresser mirror. Who is this person?

Angela has to get out of the house. She walks through empty streets to the cafe . The place is deserted. It's Saturday night. Where is everybody?

They've gone to a wedding dance in Mansfield, Dory says.

Who's getting married?

Who knows?

You mean everybody gets to go, Angela says.

You put money in the bride's shoe, Dory says.

What about you? How you doing?

I'm fine, Dory says.

I'm not, Angela says.

Told you, Dory says. You need a man.

Like a hole in the head.

You just haven't found Mr Right.

Angela buys her cigarettes and goes into the street. She breathes in the warm spring air.

That night, Angela can't fall to sleep. Finally, she gets a few hours of sleep before she has to get up for school. She takes a cold shower to wake up. Dries her chopped hair with her hair dryer.

Wait. It's Sunday. She goes back to bed. Dreams she's trying to get back home but the roads are snowed in.

11

Monday morning. She pours herself a coffee and sits down under the window in the staff room. Hawkins is in good form. He talks about the Roughriders signing a new quarterback.

Somehow Angela drags herself through the day. In her art, classes she wants her students to draw their superheros. As a child, she herself drew her princess warrior in full jewelled armour and sword, standing atop the hill, flags blowing in the wind, before battle down in the valley of death. But then her mother didn't like the mess in her eight-year old's bedroom. Her drawings, pencil crayons strewn on the floor. Her squished up paper from drawings that didn't work out. Her rocks. So her room was cleaned out. In her diary, she wrote: Guess I'm not going to be an artist.

She never told her parents how, at school, she was bullied because she had to wear thick glasses and she couldn't breathe through her stuffed-up nose. She had to breathe through her open mouth, which made her look like an idiot, even though she got high grades.

After school, Angela is walking back to her room. Simone pulls up in her car and stops. Wanna a lift?

Angela gets in.

There's a party tonight, wanna come?

Angela says she can't be seen partying with my students.

Since when did you care about their stupid rules?

I don't want to get fired.

Loosen up, Simone says. You won't get fired. I'll pick you up after supper.

Angela gets out of the car. She's missed supper. A red sun is slowly sinking down into the distant hills.

She goes into the house. Mrs Briggs isn't home. Ladies Aid probably. The women want to shut down the pool hall.

Angela heats up the casserole left by Mrs Briggs in the fridge. She takes her plate up to her room to eat. Then she lies down, exhausted from a day of teaching. She dreams she is running from a shadowy figure following her in the dark. She can't see him but he's there. She can hear him breathing. She wakes up. Takes a deep breath. Exhales. She goes to the washroom. Maybe she will go with Simone. Better than being alone. She bathes. And gets dressed in a skirt and top. She digs out the denim jacket she bought in the town's Five'nDime Store. She blow dries her hair. She is definitely going to chop it off. She gets her scissors and attacks her hair, cutting off clumps of long hair. She combs down her hair over her face and cuts bangs. She looks in the mirror. She looks different. No more sweetness and light. Raw. Don't mess with me.

There's a knock down at the door. Angela goes down and opens the door. Simone wants to know what she's done to herself?

Do you like it?

Yeah, Simone says. You look like you're ready to rock.

They get in Simone's car. They cross the railway tracks and head north of town on the grid into the coming prairie night. Simone likes to speed. Angela steels herself.

When is the last time you've had any fun?

Angela doesn't remember. She lights a cigarette with the cigarette lighter in the dashboard. A small red light under the dashboard glows on her muddy shoes. She misses the paved streets in the city. She misses the city. The streetcars. The noise of the traffic. The crowds on the sidewalks shopping. Stopping for an ice cream cone on a park bench. A guitar man busking on the street corner.

Can a girl tell another girl she wants her to make love to her?

I dunno. I've never been asked, Angela says.

Simone turns right on an east-west grid and climbs into the black, humpbacked hills against the night sky. The stars are out in full force. Simone winds through the bottom of the hills. They come into a farmyard, dark except for the lights in a large, wood-framed farmhouse. Angela gets out into the mixed smells of straw, mud and manure.

Glenda comes to the door in her red party dress and nylon-stocking feet, her lipstick a thick red. Where you been?

Simone enters the house, leaving her boots on. Who's here?

Absolutely everybody, Glenda says. Help yourself to a drink. She scoots back into the living room.

In the kitchen, Simone pours her and Angela a rum and coke. They are greeted by Gerald. Couldn't stay away, huh?

I would've if I thought you were going to be here, Simone says. She leaves Angela in the kitchen with Gerald.

Didn't expect to see you here, Gerald says.

I have no idea why I'm here, Angela says.

Because you're not a square like the other teachers.

I'll probably get fired.

Wanna dance?

Yeah.

They go into the living room and dance to Presley's Little Sister.

You like Elvis?

Everybody loves Elvis.

I'm more into Chuck Berry and Little Richard.

I like them too.

I bet you like Patsy Cline.

The most-est, Angela says.

Yeah, I like her too.

The record stops. Glenda is making out with a guy Gerald hasn't seen before. Probably from Mansfield.

Richard is slumped on the floor in the corner to the right of the picture window, very drunk. Simone, her feet under her, is perched in an armchair surveying the crowd. Gerald wants to know if Angela wants to get out of the noise.

And do what?

Go have a couple of beers. Howl at the moon.

Get me pregnant.

Why not? We could get married, start a family.

I don't think so, Angela says.

Why not?

I can't see myself living here the rest of my life.

We could go wherever you want.

You don't need somebody like me, Angela says. You need somebody like Emily, who will have your children.

Don't you want children?

No, Angela says. Definitely not. What if they turned out like me?

What's wrong with you?

Everything.

I don't see anything wrong with you.

You don't know me.

You don't want me to know you.

No, she says.

Why not?

You don't want to know.

I'm gonna have my grade twelve by the end of the month. Wasn't for the Hawkins I would've had to quit school and get a job. You see my mother, Dolly, she's the town whore. She's never wanted me around. Grandma raised me. But she's gone. I'm on my own. The Hawkins have me over for supper so that I have one square meal a day.

The Hawkins?

Yeah, Hawkins.

The cynic?

It's an act, Gerald says.

Just when you think you know people.

I have some beer, he says.

You want to get me fired?

I won't tell if you won't, he says. He drives out the exhibition grounds and parks behind the grandstand where he opens a couple of beer.

As a kid, Angela says, she loved to go the matinee grandstand and watch the magician. Once, because, the day before, she had seen the magician's trick switching the cups around and asking the audience which cup had the bean. Angela told him. Afterwards, she felt bad because it was cheating.

Gerald says he liked going to the horse races.

Why do you play the clown at school?

Maybe I don't want people finding out what I'm really like?

What are you really like?

I dunno, he says.

You more intelligent than you let on.

What good is it going to do me? I'm gonna end digging ditches like the old man.

You could get a trade, Angela says.

How'm I gonna get to the city to get a trade? Where am I gonna stay? I don't have anybody in the city.

What about starting up your business?

I wouldn't mind getting into photography, advertising. But I can't afford the price of a good camera to get started. It's a pipe dream.

Doesn't have to be?

Want another beer? He pops another couple of beer.

How come everybody drinks Pilsner?

We're from the prairie, Gerald says.

So are you going to do now?

He kisses her.

Hold me, she says.

He pulls her to him, his hand, up under her skirt, caressing the inside of her thighs.

She grabs his hand. I can't.

You can't?

Don't be mad.

Why can't you?

I can't tell you. Could you take me home?

Yeah, he says. I can do that.

You're not mad.

No, I'm not mad, he says. I really wanted to fuck you though.

I'm sorry.

Don't be.

12

It's Sunday. She sleeps in. Past noon when she wakes up. She doesn't want to get out of the luxurious, warm womb of the bed. She is called from the foot of the stairs. Someone is at the door for her. Angela slips on a skirt and sweater. She pulls a comb through her hair. At the top of the stairs, she sees it is Jason. What are you doing here?

I came to see you, he says.

I'll get my coat, Angela says.

Jason waits for her in the vestibule. In her day, a young teacher like Angela is chaperoned, Mrs Briggs says. She went to church Sunday morning. She didn't sleep in.

She shuffles into the kitchen. Her kettle is boiling for tea. Angela comes down the stairs.

Aren't you glad to see me? Jason asks.

You look great, Angela says. She forgot his boyish good looks. His innocent, baby-blue eyes. His longish burnt blond hair. He shouldn't have come. She never answered his letters.

I wanted to see for myself that you're okay, he says.

I'm not okay.

He wants to know if they could find somewhere to eat. I just got off the train. God this country is dismal. Nothing but flat prairie.

I've come to love the prairie, Angela says. It calms me.

You know that I love you, Jason says.

Don't.

I can't just switch off my feelings, he says.

You don't have to save me.

I want to be with you.

Jason, she says, I don't feel the same way.

We can still be friends, he says.

No, she says. There's too much history. You have to forget me. Find a girl who wants to be with you.

I have to get something to eat, he says.

The Chinese cafe will be open, Angela says.

After they eat a breakfast of pancakes and sausages, Angela takes him out on her prairie. A duck lifts off the small slough behind the cow fence.

I miss you, Angela. Our talks. Books we've read. Movies we've gone to.

You'll find somebody.

How?

Be open.

I'll miss you.

She looks at Jason struggling with the rejection, the loss of his dreams, draining from his handsome, boyish face. He tries to hold back the tears. He turns from her so she can't see he is crying warm tears.

I'm so sorry, Angela says.

Me too.

He takes the evening train back to the city.

Angela goes up to her room and pours herself a glass of wine. That night, Angela can't sleep. She turns on the light. She starts a letter home. She has nothing to write about. For a long time, she stands at the window in her loneliness. It is raining. A car below in the street goes by. She fights the depression descending on her. She wants to die, she doesn't want to die.

13

Angela reads Wordsworth to her grade twelve class.

I wandered lonely as a cloud

That floats on high o'er vales and hills,

When all at once I saw a crowd,

A host of golden daffodils

She gives her grade eleven class an assignment to write a list of what they see out the window. What do you feel from what you see? Happy? Sad? Melancholy? Peaceful? Try writing a poem.

She goes to the staff room to get away from prying eyes. They're going to see through her, see she's nothing but white trash, a whore. They won't want to have anything to do with her. Nobody will.

She picks up a pair of scissors. Cuts at her wrists. She bleeds.

Simone has followed her. What are you doing?

I don't feel anything, Angela says.

It's okay, Simone tells her. She takes Angela into the washroom where she washes the cuts. Angela waits while Simone runs for the first aid kit. Angela looks in the mirror. She is crying. Simone returns and bandages the cuts. She takes Angela behind the school where they have a cigarette in the bright sun. Angela is very tired. Simone takes her to the house. She helps her get into bed. Angela should sleep. Simone sits in the chair, her feet crossed on the foot of the bed, her skirt caught up on her thighs.

Angela looks at Simone, who is not a child. She is an attractive young woman. Older than she should be.

I'll come back later, Simone is saying. She closes the door. Then she is gone. Angela sleeps.

In the morning, Angela wakes up, exhausted. She drags herself out of bed. Climbs into the bathtub. She falls asleep. Wakes up. The water is cold. She runs hot water. Using up the hot water. Mrs Briggs won't be happy.

Angela is going out the front door when she's stopped by Mrs Briggs. I've warned you about Simone. Stay away from that girl. She's evil. Like her mother.

Angela hates these days when she didn't get enough sleep and she has to drag herself through classes. She gives her students a writing assignment. She wants them to write their reaction to Sylvia Plath's poem, Crossing the Water: The horizons ring me like faggots,/Tilted and disparate, and always unstable...

For once, they work without making a sound. Like in a morgue. Like they sense something is wrong.

Milly comes to the teacher's desk. I don't know what I'm suppose to do, she whispers.

Write what you feel the poet is feeling.

How would I know what she's feeling?

By the words she uses. What she is saying.

It's hard, Milly says.

Nothing is ever easy.

Milly goes back to her desk. She glances at Leo.

Angela heads to the staff room for a cigarette.

Petry comes in. Becoming a habit, he says. You leaving your students alone to have a cigarette. Are you trying to kill yourself?

Angela butts her cigarette and returns to her class. Tell me, she says, why should I teach you poetry. You're not going to read poetry when you leave school. You going to get home from a job you hate and watch stupid sitcoms to fill in your little miserable lives before you go to bed.

Angela walks out of the classroom. She leaves the school, gets to her rooms and, fully dressed, climbs under her covers.

Mrs Briggs comes up to her door. Mr Petry called. He wanted to know if you're all right.

I'm having a nervous breakdown, Angela says.

He thought as much, Mrs Briggs says. He told me to tell you to take a few days off.

Angela sleeps. She wakes up and goes back to sleep. She dreams her labyrinth dreams in which she can't find her way out. She wakes up, unsettled. Depressed. Damn him. She never used to get depressed. She'd have her down days. But now, these past couple of months, she's struggled with depression. She prays for God to take away her depression so she can live a normal life. But she gets no answer.

14

Simone stops Angela in the hallway. You've heard about Gerald. He's being charged for raping Emily. He didn't but she doesn't want her father to know she's a little whore.

Gerald could go to jail, Angela says.

Exactly. The little bitch.

Emily will tell the truth.

Not likely. Not Emily.

You don't like her.

What's there to like.

Poor Gerald, Angela says.

You have a thing for him, don't you?

Don't be silly, Angela says. I'm his teacher.

You were dancing with him.

It used to be that a female teacher couldn't go out at night without a chaperone?

He was your chaperone, was he?

I thought you'd be all for women's rights.

I am.

After supper and her walk along the railway tracks, Angela stops in the cafe . Joe Willis comes over from the counter with his cup of coffee and asks if he can join her.

Your Gerald's older brother, Angela says. How is Gerald?

Not, good, Joe says. Guilty until proven innocent.

Angela orders a coffee. I can't see Gerald being guilty. Underneath the bravado, he's sweet.

Sweet?

Isn't he?

He wouldn't wanna hear you say he's sweet, Joe says.

He was doing so well in school.

He's gonna be like me and never finish high school.

But you read philosophy. David Hume. Descartes. I think, therefore, I am. About all I know. I read mostly literature. I do like Iris Murdoch. A Severed Head is a hoot. You should go back to school and teach philosophy.

I'm quite happy with my life the way it is.

I wish my life was.

You don't like teaching.

I don't like having to fight with students who don't want to learn.

I gotta get back home, Joe says. Nice talking to you. He goes out into the night.

You know Joe's a faggot, says the woman with her child at the next table says.

So what if he is?

It's not natural.

I have to tell you, Dory says, Larry's got a new job driving the truck for Liberty Transport. He will be gone most of the time, sometimes as far as the Ontario, can you believe it?

I've never been anywhere myself, Dory says. Except once, when I was a kid, my family drove to Sault Saint Marie to visit my mom's half-sister. who'd been left on an aunt's farm because mom's step-mother didn't want to have to look after a baby in the west where people lived in mud huts. So the two half-sisters grew up separately. Mom's half-sister did all the farm chores and housework while her aunt sat in the kitchen by the stove and gossiped with her neighbours.

Mom's step-mother never liked my mom. At fourteen, mom was sent to be the housekeeper on the Olson farm. At sixteen, she was married to the hired man and they moved into town where he got a job in the tire shop. So me and my brother grew up in town.

And you've never left.

Everybody else has. My best friend, Maggie, teaches in a big city school. Her brother is a big city lawyer. Both have never married.

There's a story about my great grandfather, Angela says. He and his brother were identical twins. Even their wives couldn't tell them apart. So the twins would sleep with each other's wives. When it came out, the wives made my great-grandfather grow a moustache.

Dory wants to know if Angela knows Mr Cox has a son, Fenton. You must have seen him bombing around town in his little red convertible. All show. Anyway, he was going out with Jennifer's older sister, Marlene, knocking her up. Fenton's mother wasn't having her son wasting his life marrying white trash. So the Cox's paid off Marlene's parents.

What happened to Marlene?

From what I heard. Dory says, the baby was stillborn.

So all for nothing, Angela says.

I don't know if you know the post mistress' son, Bart Thompson. She's very religious. The wages of sin is death and all that. I don't think I've ever seen her smile. Anyway Bart hanged out with Fenton. From what I heard, Fenton and Bart, from the trees, spied on Mrs Cox, who still has her figure, sunbathing in the nude behind the farm house. Probably spent the afternoon getting horny and jerking off if I know what guys are like. And I know. Like I wasn't more than fifteen that my cousin, Freddy, got me drunk in the back seat of his dad's car where he got into me.

You're lucky he didn't get you pregnant.

The problem is that when a girl gets it, she wants more. God, how I worried every month until I got my period.

I should go, Angela says.

You know Cox's daughter, Fiona was shacked up with an asshole in the city. They got into fight so he left, drunk, got into the car and plowed into a streetlamp. There was brain damage so, I guess, she felt she couldn't leave him. Like it was her fault starting a fight with him. I guess looking after him and going to university was hard. So, from what I hear, she dropped out of university, got a waitress job to pay for the rent and food and his medical care and booze. I mean, for chrissakes, the asshole was leeching off her.

Why does she put up with him?

I haven't the faintest idea coz, as I've heard he likes to throw her around. One time they got into a fight and he threw her and she hit her head on the corner of the cupboard. He could've killed her.

How long as this been going on?

I dunno. The accident was sometime last year. He didn't have suffer severe brain damage. But he was not going back to work, the asshole was leeching off her.

But she's come back home, traumatized, scared shitless of the asshole will come after her. She'd come in here to buy cigarettes. I've never seen somebody change like her. Like I mean she was daddy's sweet little girl. Now she's a foul-mouthed slut. God, the way she puts people down. Like she called me a fat-ass bitch coz I didn't make fresh coffee for her. And there were stories she would get a guy here in the beer parlour to buy her drinks. Then piss him off by going out to his best friend's place. Probably fucking him.

There were friends fighting in the beer parlour. Which meant nothing to her. Like she drains the blood out of men and then spits them out. A femme fatale.

Angela pays for her coffee and goes out into the grey street. An old long bearded man in a denim smock and pants and old boots is pissing in the dead grass along the wall of the Royal Bank.

You're the poet, Angela says.

Pissing in the wind.

Your poems tell us where we came from. What it means to be a prairie-person. We're to help others. How, in the beginning, our home were built. First out of poplar poles and straw bale roofs. The lumber hewed out fir trees. How farmers helped each other at harvest. We were to put back in what we took out of the world. It's what built this country.

Those days are long gone, he says. Nowadays, it's all about me. Be myself. Hitler was being himself.

Still you shouldn't worry about what other people think of you.

I'd never been a poet if I had worried what people were going to think of me when I was putting myself out there.

I'm glad you did.

I was happy back then. But happiness doesn't last long. It's a battle to put food on the table. I should've been like my brother and gone into law.

Angela lights a cigarette.

You're going to kill yourself,

I'm gonna quit, Angela says. Tomorrow.

Tomorrow never comes.

Simone comes out of the beauty parlour. You like my hair? Want a ride?

Angela says she prefers to walk. She loves the silence as the sun sets and the day closes down.

In her room, she doesn't turn on the light in the coming darkness. Something dark about Simone. Dangerous. The surge of electricity in her dark eyes. A power pulling Angela in. She's been warned to stay away from Simone.

She opens a bottle of wine. She must do something about the bottles piling up under her bed.

In the morning, the sun is warm. The dandelions spread their yellow carpet on the edge of the summerfallow across the railway tracks. A hawk circles against the blue sky. She should write a poem.

School has settled into a routine. Classes come and go. Somehow Angela gets through the day and walks uptown to buy cigarettes. You've heard, Dory says, that Emily confessed Gerald didn't rape her. I didn't think she'd let him go to jail.

I thought her father was going to kill her.

She was wrong about her father. All he said was that he was happy she wasn't pregnant. Even so, Gerald has taken off to the oil fields in Alberta.

He had so much wanted to get his grade twelve, Angela says. What he could've made of himself.

How life never works out the way we want, Karen says, hurrying home to get supper on.

Angela wonders what her mother wanted to be and didn't get the chance. She never said. Or her dad selling sewing machines for a living. Out on the road all week alone. What kind of life is that?

After supper with Mrs Briggs, Angela goes to the library. She finds her friend there. What happened?

I walked into the door.

You didn't walk into a door.

I'm alright.

You have to leave him, Angela says, before he kills you.

What do you know about it? What makes you think you know everything? Think you're so smart, you can come in here and tell me how to run my life. He's a good man, He's not perfect. Nobody is.

Angela wants to help. She can't. Becky's in denial. She stays. Like she's addicted to him. She can't leave him. He hits her, says he's sorry, then the sex, the fix. It's classic.

You don't understand, Becky is saying. You don't know him. When he walks into a room everybody looks up to him. What he says goes. He could've had any girl he wanted, but he chose me. You know what that meant. I was somebody. The other girls were jealous I was wearing his high school jacket. We got married. Then things started to go wrong. He lost his job when the packing plant shut down. You don't know what that was like. You got an education. You can easily find a job. Different for him. Months and no work. He started getting down on himself. Took it out on me. Everything was my fault.

Angela watches as her friend buttons her coat and leaves the library. No. She doesn't understand. She wants there to be a god she can pray to, a god who will save her friend from the hell she chooses to live in. But there is no god. All that's left is the cold, indifferent silence of the universe.

Simone visits Angela. She looks through the drawings on the dresser. These are good, she says. Angela offers her a glass of wine. I like them.

You should, Simone says. They're very strong.

They make me feel strong.

You are strong.

No, I'm not, Angela says.

Simone sits beside Angela on the bed. What's wrong?

You don't want to know, Angela says.

I want to know everything, Simone says.

I was raped, Angela says.

Jesus, Simone says. She covers Angela with kisses, my poor sweet darling.

I should've gone to the police. Fought back.

They would've done fuck all. Except drag you through shit.

Why me? Had he been observing me? That I sat off by myself in the lunch room? I had no friends. He must have thought I was an easy target.

What in heaven's name is going on here! It's Mrs Briggs. Her bulk in the doorway, blocking escape from the odour of her self-righteousness. Thought there was something going on between the two of you.

15

A grey, windy morning, Angela waits for the train. Mr Cox waits with her. Don't be too hard on us, he says.

Part II

16

Angela gets off the two-fifteen train in the prairie city of Saskatoon, June twenty-ninth. She doesn't want her family back in the Queen City to know where she is. The family will be upset. Especially Christine. How could Angela cut herself off? Not that Christine would have had anything to do with Angela. Even back in high school, Christine had her own clique of bubblegum mamas who, after school, hung out in the Chinese cafe , gossiping about who was going with whom while Angela went home to do her homework before supper. Christine boogied along on her pursuit of happiness. Her life a cliche. Finish school. Get a job, find a man. Get married, have children. Volunteer at the soup kitchen and then congratulate herself she is saving the world.

Unlike Christine, Angela is a loner, the introvert, struggling with the black dogs of depression, being careful she doesn't do anything wrong like getting staggering drunk in public so she won't suffer the dread that weighs her down with the fear she will be punished, humiliated. To protect herself, if she can, she sticks to herself, avoiding people by carrying in her shoulder bag a notebook and second hand paperbacks of poetry and modernist novels like Sound and Fury and Margaret Avison's poetry.

Even now, on sunny days, Angela can be seen sitting on the green grass of the city park, reading or sketching with water colours.

Now a days, in Saskatoon, structuralism is big, but Angela is still painting her open prairie landscapes into which she can escape from the inner turmoil in her soul.

Even so, she's searching through library books to find a way out of her depression. How as a child, she was wired by her mother's disapproval. Her constant criticism. Angela couldn't do anything right. Even now, in her head, she hears her mother's voice scolding her. Go put on matching coloured socks. Close you mouth. You look like a retard.

Angela, at fourteen, asked her father why her mother hated her.

Don't be silly, he said. She loves you. You're her daughter.

Hated by her mother is why Angela seeks approval from people. But like with her mother, she won't get approval. So she tells herself to hell with it and rebels. She cuts off her hair, which she pushes back into a ducktail like the boys.

She won't do what people want. She's not going to let her mother's voice run her life, be controlled. She's not a bad, stupid person. Enough with the self-contempt. She doesn't need approval. They don't give a crap about her, they've got their own little lives to worry about. Think they can't be wrong. They're right and she's wrong. She should shut the fuck up.

She wishes she was dead. Stop the awful dread that people will find out she's been raped. Blaming her. Her fault. She was asking for it. The humiliation.

So damn naive going up to Jonathan's studio to see his paintings. She thought Jonathan was a friend. But she now sees that being from University Park, he saw her, as she was from the wrong part of town, a piece of white trash whom he could have if he wanted.

Who was going to believe her? He knows it's his word against the little slut from the wrong part of town.

And now fired. Nothing about her privacy being invaded by a respected member of the community. No no no. The pride of the self-righteous. They're so perfect.

Okay, done. She can take control of her life, no idiot principal calling her into his office lecturing her. But first, she needs a room. Then a drink.

She takes a room in the King George, dropping off her suitcase and going back down to the street where she asks a panhandler where she can find a government liquor board store. Couple of blocks east, then hang a right, he says.

She makes her way on the cracked sidewalks. Finds the liquor board store and buys a couple of cheap bottles of red wine. She stops in a five-and-dime and buys a scribbler and pencils. Up in her room, she pours herself a glass of wine and starts on a self-obsessed self-portrait.

From the classifieds, she finds a room a few blocks from off Broadway near the river.

She finds the house address. The room is in the attic with sloping ceilings, cot, small electric stove, fridge, a few pots and pans, dishes, bathroom down the hallway. She pays a month's rent and, at the Econo, buys wieners and buns, couple of bananas and a bag of rice, coffee. She hauls her grocery bags up to her attic rooms and unpacks. She pours herself a vodka and Pepsi. She starts on a poem to exorcise her demons. Self-pity, really. Not good.

To get out of herself, she starts to write a short story that isn't about her. She writes about a young poet who rebels against his Christian parents. He's a poet, who calls himself Baal, after the whoring god of the ancient Canaanites. He becomes involved with an older, married woman, who takes him to bed. But that's all he wants to do. She tries ending it with him and he rapes her, knowing she won't call the police for fear her husband finding out about her and her fifteen year old lover.

She mails the manuscript to the Prairie Prism literary magazine. She receives a rejection letter. Prairie Prism doesn't print violence. So her story of violence against women goes unpublished. She should mail the story to the magazine, Counter. They, not the city newspaper, printed the story about a woman on the reservation being brutally raped by her husband. She wanted to call the RCMP. But her family stopped her. They didn't want the outside world to know that violence against women is a reality on reservations. They want the public to believe in the European noble savage myth that the tribes live in harmony with mother earth.

Angela goes back to writing her self-obsessed poetry in the tradition of Sylvia Plath. She joins a reading circle and becomes friends with a Nathan Collier, a poet in his forties. She likes his poems of the prairie landscape and the people, struggling to make a living in the dust bowl of the dirty thirties, good people and bad people, bandits and con artists, who made life worse. He wrote about the wanted Billy Warton, who was not mourned when he died in a gun battle with the police in the southern bad lands. In another poem, he told the story of the Frog Lake Massacre where a band of Cree attacked and killed nine officials, clergy and settlers in the small settlement.

Angela goes back to painting her self-portraits, which are becoming more expressionist as she works out her inner demons. She joins an art group and becomes friends with a Michal Dabrowski, a young artist in university, who is painting fauvist prairie landscapes with his sad-sack purple and orange cows against green green of home under white, puffy clouds floating in the eternal blue sky.

He says that he paints the coloured cows as an escape from his short stories and plays, which are full of conflict and violence. He wrote a short play in which a fellow traveller, a retired high school principal, in an isolated train station, is tormented by a punk and his sister. The punk makes the school principal get on his knees so the punk can ride him, pulling his ears until the old man screams like a piggy. The punk kills the old man to see what it's like.

Angela finds a job as a waitress in a coffee shop on Broadway. She soon finds that the owner runs the place like a warden.

It's not just you she gets on, the waitresses say. They hate to say it but some women can be real bitches. Angela walks out.

17

Angela stops in for a beer. The beer parlour is air-conditioned. It wasn't that long ago women couldn't go into beer parlours. Then it was okay if they were escorted to the section segregated for women. The law has finally caught up to the fact women are human beings in their own right. Wow, they even get the vote.

Friends in the art group catch up to her at home to tell her that Michal attempted suicide and ended up in the psych ward where he was diagnosed schizophrenic because he told the psychiatrist that he heard voices telling him he was no good, he should kill.

Angela visits Michal who tells her he was given shock treatments, which left him disorientated, he didn't know which way to go. To go home or run away.

Angela tells him she has to get him out of the psyche ward. Once he's been labelled schizophrenic, he can't get away from the label.

How do you know that?

Because I was diagnosed schizophrenic, which proved mom right, I was the problem. All I wanted was her approval, which I'm never going to get. But, unconsciously, I'm still wanting her approval, for her to tell me she loves me. I was fourteen, I asked father why does mother hate me. He said, Don't be silly, she loves you.

But a kid knows, right?

She was always on me. I didn't want to wear dresses. I had to wear glasses. I couldn't breathe through my nose so my mouth was always open. Mother told me to close my mouth, I looked like a retard. But I wasn't, I was smart, creative. I even skipped a grade.

Then father, drunk, sitting at the kitchen table, rolling cigarettes for the next day, told me he wasn't my father. Mom was pregnant when he married her. So all those years growing up, wasn't me. Mom hated me because I reminded her she'd been a whore. Which she took out on me. I grew up feeling there was something wrong with me.

Angela goes back to her rooms and changes into clean jeans and blouse, pulls on her denim jacket and leaves for the evening poetry reading in the Gaia Coffeehouse. She is going to read her poem protesting the jailing of Martin Luther King Jr. His speech: I had a dream.

After she comes down from the stage, a visiting poet from the Toronto coffeehouse scene climbs on stage and berates his bourgeois audience for expecting poetry to express reality. It's not reality. It's a string of words making up its own realty. A reality of nothingness. Things don't happen for a reason. Things don't get better. Love does not conquer all. Working hard doesn't get you ahead. People are not basically good. We're all deluding ourselves. Life is the shits and then we die.

18

Angela gets a part-time job reading manuscripts for a local publishing house, Riverside Publishing. To supplement her income, she paints flowers in decorative vases. She's working on a short story in which Florence finds a phone number on a piece of paper in her husband, Franklin's suit jacket pocket. She shows his brother, Teddy, who staying with them while he looks for work. He holds her in his arms. Kisses her on the mouth. Florence feels the warmth of being loved. She takes his hand and leads him to his bedroom where, kissing, they fall on the bed. He is tender with her as his cock fills her with beloved. But later that night, feeling guilty Teddy confesses to Franklin that he fucked his wife. Franklin kicks

Florence out. She's left to fend for herself on the streets in a whole new world of pimps, petty thieves, drug dealers, struggling to survive in an uncaring world. She turns to selling herself to buy drugs to numb herself enough to keep living a hopeless life where nobody gave a shit for her.

Angela goes back to painting, working on a series of landscapes. After several months, she has enough for a show. Sheila Durmid, who owns the Avant Garde Gallery, agrees to stop in Angela's studio and look at her paintings. She finally shows up. Does Angela not know about the Regina Five and their move into abstraction. Angela tries explaining that painting her prairie landscapes, like the prairie itself, heals her. But Sheila is having none of it. Besides, Angela's brushwork is clumsy. Too visible.

19

In her box of stuff, Angela finds the photo she took from the family album. The photo is of her father as a young man in the beer parlour, sitting at a table with his drinking buddies: Harrison, a welder, who never married; Harold Brown, who got by doing odd jobs around the neighbourhood on the south side. And Farley, a warehouse lift operator, who lived in the beer parlour to escape a nagging wife and five kids fighting over who's job it was to wash dishes.

Sad, really. Ordinary lives. Never really getting anywhere. Hard work. Few pleasures. Except a draft of beer with friends.

20

The depression is bad. She can barely get out of bed. She was never depressed before she was raped. The antidepressant medication isn't working. She is dragging herself through the day. Some days she doesn't get out of bed. She doesn't eat. Drinks a bottle of wine.

Can't go on like this. She has to get back to painting. Get up like she does and first thing, with her coffee, write. Something will come to her. Always does. Write down a sentence. "Who took the last of the coffee? "Now what? Who did? Who is upset? What are they to each other? Mother/daughter? Worker/co-worker? There's a story in there.

21

Her sister, Christine, all dolled up in bright, yellow dress, matching earrings and high heels, shows up at Angela's room. How can you live like this?

Like what?

Look at the mess. A dumpy bed. Does the electric stove even work?

A couple of burners.

Why the martyrdom?

I'm doing what I want, Angela says.

No respect for yourself.

Are you happy, Christine?

I have my days. Eddie is good to me. Get dressed, I'm taking you out to eat.

While waiting for Angela to change into a skirt, Christine picks up the book Life Against Death.

Why do you want to read this stuff for? Bunch of losers. It's depressing. She throws the book into the garbage. You need to get a life.

I have a life, Angela says.

I mean in the real world.

Says the woman nobody knows what she looks like under all the makeup.

Christine laughs. Barbie doesn't have to grow up, remember.

They go down to the street where Christine unlocks the doors to her red Impala. Nice, eh?

Brand new?

Yep.

I was told, Angela says, that there's a new Chinese place out on Eighth Street. You're okay with Chinese?

I love Chinese, Christine says. Tell me, what have you been up to? As if I don't know. I read somewhere that your chances of making it in art are about the same as being struck by lightning.

I paint because I have to, Angela says. It's who I am.

Still it would be good to make some money so you could get yourself a decent place to live. You haven't asked about mom and dad.

How are mom and dad?

The same. Mom never listens. Dad has to repeat what he says. The third time, he raises his voice so he can be heard. Then he gets scolded for raising his voice.

They will never change, Angela says.

You got a guy?

Why would I want a guy?

Sex.

I don't need a guy pestering me for sex.

You know that I'm working as a receptionist in an insurance office. It's great. I have to go into the boss's office to take dictation. Afterwards, he likes to bend me over his desk and lift my skirt, pull down my panties and shag me like a billy-goat. Don't tell Eddie.

Why would I tell Eddie?

I dunno, Christine says. To get back at me.

For what?

For not being a good sister to you.

And what should a good sister be?

I dunno, Christine says.

Me neither.

You're not coming home, are you?

I'm okay here.

I don't have to worry about you offing yourself?

Why would you worry?

I'm your sister.

Her sister puts on so much makeup, nobody knows what she really looks like. So inauthentic. But it's the made-up self that makes it in society. Christine plays her barbie-doll role. Angela being the rebel.

After lunch, all Christine wants to do is go shopping. She tries on a dress, twirls on her high heels. What do you think?

You look great.

I don't want to get old, Christine says. Perish the thought.

She doesn't buy the dress. Let's go, she says. In the street, a male passerby gives her a second look. Christine looks back at him, pleased with herself.

Angela wants to get far away from the madding crowd in the downtown core.

I don't blame you for not wanting to come back home, Christine says. I mean with mom's long suffering martyrdom, dad resigned to his miserable life. Like a morgue around the house. And me and Eddie are fighting like cats and dogs.

You're always fighting, Angela says.

Maybe I start fighting so nobody can get close to me. Why do you go around in those dumpy clothes?

Maybe I don't want anybody to get close to me.

Angela is tired, she wants her sister's voice to stop. But it won't stop. It's like she has to hear the sound of her own voice to confirm she exists.

22

Angela knows she's never going to fit into the art scene. She knows artists who know people who get them shows, but she hates brown-nosing. It's politics and she wants to paint and write. It's outrageous how women are treated. How they're shunted. If women do get a show, they're paid far less than the males.

At a coffee shop poetry reading, this woman said she liked Angela's poems. They speak to the injustices women have to live with.

She invited Angela to sit with her and her husband, Heath, a tall, good-looking man with blues eyes that go along with blondish hair, who teaches English at the university. She herself teaches grade five. Her name is Phyllis, a small woman with a soft-white face, fragile.

Angela, over the months, run into them and they stop for coffee. They all bitch about the cold spring weather. Heath wants to talk about Khrushchev sending nuclear weapons to Cuba. Be a good thing if the communists wiped out America.

You haven't read Solzhenitsyn. Or you'd know, under communism, to keep your mouth shut because if you spoke about about the loss of human rights, you be tried in a kangaroo court and shot, buried in mass graves in the forests, or sent to the gulags.

So you're a capitalist.

Yeah, right. I'm living on the hog.

Wasn't long, Phyllis stops in to see Angela. Heath read a letter he got from a married woman, telling him to bugger off. You have to read between lines, he says. She's torn between being married and attracted to me. She's always showing up, wanting to go for coffee.

Andela wants to know what Phyllis is going to do.

I dunno. Heath wants an open marriage.

Do you?

I tried. One night, I went over to the apartment of one of Heath's university friends, Jonas Moore. I'd seen him before. He wasn't what you'd call good-looking. But he was a gentle man, soft-spoken. His wife had flown to the west coast to be with her dying mother.

When I got home after midnight, Heath was waiting up for me. I turned on living room light on. What are you doing sitting in the dark?

How did it go?

Nothing happened.

What do you mean nothing happened?

We drank a bit of wine. Talked.

About what?

Nothing really.

Nothing?

He was not happy in his marriage. Felt trapped.

But you did go to bed.

Yeah, but nothing happened.

Nothing happened?

To be honest, he couldn't get it up.

Heath laughs. He couldn't get it up.

What pisses me off, she says, I could've fucked around. There were guys hitting on me. But I was married. Stupid me.

You still can.

I'm too old.

So you're stuck with Heath.

Guess I am, Phyllis says and rushes home.

Angela can hear her clickety-clack down the stairs.

23

Angela feels bad that she's been avoiding Phyllis. Coming out of the corner store, she runs into Phyllis. She tries to give her a hug but Phyllis says she doesn't mean it. You think you're being nice, but you're not. You're not being authentic.

She goes on about her and Heath not talking. They have nothing to say anymore, nothing in common. On top of everything, her pottery isn't selling.

Angela says she's has to get back to her painting. She hurries away, tired of being dumped on. She feels like shit. But it's not her fault the two aren't getting along, that her pottery isn't selling.

She gets back home, puts the coffee on, looks at her gesso-ed canvas on the easel. There's nothing to paint. Rows of soup cans. Everything the same. Who's to judge what's good, what's bad? To be radical would be not to paint. But then who would know? She'd have to write a manifesto and post it around the city. Instead, she cleans her brushes, changes into her paint clothes, pours herself a coffee, lights a cigarette, stares at the canvas. Like back in university, she should rip up coloured paper, glue them to the canvas where they fall. Then splash runny paint on the coloured paper. This time, she could use a straw and blow the paint around. Voila. Her art professor had been ecstatic when she showed him her piece. Maybe she should go back and play around with colour.

She changes back into street clothes, grabs her bag and walks to the edge of the city. She loves the prairie, the vast horizons, the blue sky. She can let herself go and breathe.

She stands in her loose white, virgin dress, against the prairie wind, arms straight out, like a cross, wanting the wind to bring the prairie spirit to wash through her, wash out the evil spirits that fill her body with dread. Free her. So she can live.

24

She stares at the white canvas. What is there left to paint? Everything has been said. She cleans her pallet knives. Changes into a top and jeans. Grabs her bag of paperbacks and sketch books and descends to the street. She heads straight for the coffee shop at the top of the bridge. The sun is hot. She should have brought a brimmed hat.

It is cool inside the coffee shop. She orders a cup of coffee and grabs a newspaper, taking a seat at a table against the windows which overlook the street. She feels she's being stared at. She glances at the wall to her right where a blue-eyed, greying beard, long-haired older guy, maybe even in his fifties. He is dressed in working class plaid shirt, jeans, and work boots is staring at her.

Didn't your mom tell you it isn't nice to stare?

He picks up his coffee, comes over and takes a seat at her table. I'm going to take you to bed, he wants.

You think so.

I know so.

Do you mind if I finish my coffee first?

Take your time.

I will, she says, sipping her coffee. He isn't what she would call good looking. But there is a strength in his face and body. A magnetism. Like she'd be safe in his bear hug. But she doesn't want to be in love. It's crazy. Why get tied down? Lose her independence. Love makes her feel. To want. And she doesn't want to want. It can be taken from her.

I see paint on your hands. You're an artist.

I like to call myself an artist.

I paint. Abstract expressionism.

How come I haven't seen you around?

Busy setting up a studio here to get away from the primadonnas in the Ontario art scene. Name's Karl. Your name's Angela Kovak. Your friend Ellis has told me all about you.

I don't even know all about me.

He was right, you're an angel.

I'm no angel.

Angela feels the fear she will be swallowed up, devoured. Nothing left of her. But she can't be like her mother, afraid of life. Never venturing from the house. A constant battle against the filth in the house. Everyday changing the soiled bed sheets. On guard against salmonella and e. coli. The vegetables washed and scrubbed, blemishes cut out, thrown into the garbage. The slightest sign of spoilage and the food thrown out. A person can never be too careful. The threat of botulism, of death. Her fear of death.

She shouldn't but she goes to Karl's studio where he's working on a huge canvas of abstract colours of paint.

You have a lot of rage inside you, she says.

Look at the world, the shit and corruption which people like us have to put up with.

25

The morning is drenched in a bright sun coming through the studio windows. She can smell Karl on the mattress, his hairy animal smell. the smell of turpentine and oil paint and stale cigarettes and sour wine left in the bottom of bottles on the floor.

You're awake.

I think so, he says.

Good morning.

Is it?

Angela makes coffee while he showers and comes to the kitchen table. I want to get an early start in the studio, he says.

I'm gonna stay here and paint.

He downs his coffee. See you later. He pounds down the stairs in his heavy boots.

Angela gets dressed in her paint clothes. Pours herself a strong coffee and sits at her easel and gessos the blank canvas. Can she pull off a painting? Pull what off?

All the masses want are paintings of grain elevators and railway tracks and wild horses running in the foothills.

She was told she has to feel the painting on the canvas. Feel what? The turmoil in her body? The anxiety?

Calm herself. She can't. Her brain is racing on about her dread that people will find out she was raped.

She starts by layering a strip of blue across the horizon. Yellow. Orange. Blue. Purple. Yellow again. Fill in the rest of the sky with a darkening purple. A thick green-black wall of trees.

Still there is the compulsion to paint, write, to work out why she's feeling bad, her shame. How can she get herself to start feeling better. Maybe then she can't. But it wasn't her, it was him. He raped her. He should be made to suffer. But she doesn't have brothers to cut his balls off with the jagged edge of tin can lid. So he gets to go on with his life like nothing happened. Not to him. Just another conquest. He can brag to his friends Angela was a lovely piece. How they must look at her like she was nothing but a whore. Maybe they could get into her her. Christ. That's how she's seen. How she feels she's seen. How can she live like that? Being seen. Being looked at. How does Karl see her?

She can't know what someone is thinking. Be awful if he sees her as nothing but a lovely piece. Surely not. But how could she know for sure? He holds her like he cares for her. Feels like it. He is tender with her being a big man. Talks to her like she has a brain. Maybe he doesn't know.

She can't stop thinking of her rapist. How she could kill him. Pretend she's glad to see him. Give him a big hug and shove a shiv up into his heart.

She doesn't want to feel like that. She wants to feel good about life.

Angela is feeling restless, agitated. Damn Karl. Why did he have to come into her life? What if he finds out she was raped? Contaminated? Even if he loves her, it will be there, stuck in his gut.

But then Karl shows up, takes a shower, dresses, opens a beer, sits at the kitchen table as Angela peels potatoes for supper. She asks him if he was ever married.

It was a mistake, he says. He and his wife were two desperate kids wanting to be loved.. Both suffering depression. Dumping on each other to feel better. Sucking the life-force out of the other. In the end, he left. A couple of friends let him sleep in their basement. He didn't bother them. Bought his own food. Until the divorce. His daughter told him mom called him a bastard. But she remarried. So she's okay. His daughter married young.

You ever see her?

She so much wants a baby. But hubby is sterile.

Angela's not sure she wants to fall in love. So scared she'd be needy. Then there's the anxiety love can be taken away. She and her abandonment issues.

No, she doesn't want the obligation, the demands of love, wears a person out. Like her father, all those years, heading out on the road to get respite from a nagging wife.

26

It's late when Karl gets back. She shouldn't have waited up for him. But she couldn't sleep. Karl comes to her.

Phyllis was here, she says.

Don't get pulled in, Karl says. There's nothing you can do. Up to her.

She's gone over the edge, Angela says.

And what? She might commit suicide?

She might.

And you have to save her?

I can't, Angela says.

Phyllis has to get what she wants. I can't believe we're talking about her. Nothing's going to change. She is going to stay with Phillip. If she leaves the asshole, she would have nobody to blame she's never got anywhere herself. Nothing's her fault. God is punishing her. Look at the attention she gets. Poor Phyllis having to put up with Phillip. Don't you just feel sorry for her.

I worry about her.

Don't. All it does is make you feel bad. And you don't have to feel bad. There is nothing you can do.

27

Christine says she ran into Damien. He's married. Did Angela know? His wife's name's Simone. He's in real estate.

I need to know that, Angela says.

Look, it happened. Move on.

Easy for you to say. You've never been raped.

I love fucking, Chrstine says. But I wish men would learn a woman doesn't appreciate being jack-hammered. Like slow down. Whisper sweet-nothings in her ear.

28

Karl is ready to give up painting. I can't find what I'm looking for.

Go back to figures for a while.

You'll pose for me?

Not likely.

So you'd be okay if I hired models.

Do what you want.

What if I fuck them?

I don't want to know about it.

I don't want to fuck them, I want to fuck you.

Not right now, I'm making supper. Sausage cooked in cabbage.

I'll go get a six-pack.

Great idea.

Karl had come from the bush country where he grew up the baby in a family of twelve. Us ragamuffins, he says, slept on a big mattress on the floor of a granary. You wanted to make sure you pissed before you crawled into bed because if you got up to go piss (a full moon, forty below night freeze the balls off a brass monkey) you lost your warm body spot in the middle of the mattress. At the table when the food came round the table you took as much you could get away with. Mostly filled up on potatoes. Father and his brothers hunted so we ate deer, mouse, elk, bear. We ate a lot of fish. And vegetables from the garden. In the fall, we stuffed our mouths with saskatoon and blue berries and what we could grab from raiding gardens. We drank from the cows. Wines from dandelions and goldenrod. Booze from the stills.

29

An old woman enters Angela's dream. Angela can't see her face. I don't know who you are, Angela says. The woman says it doesn't matter. All she wants is to bum a cigarette.

Angela bums her a cigarette.

The old woman wants to know what unpardonable sin Angela has committed that she can't be forgiven.

I didn't ask to be raped.

You have to forgive him.

He doesn't think he did anything wrong. I didn't mean no.

Angela wakes up. She needs a shot of vodka. Calm the rage inside her.

She should be like Christine and go shopping.

Angela can't sleep. All her life she has suffered insomnia. Maybe she should become a lady-of-the-night. Earn some extra cash.

She goes out into the night and wanders down to the river's edge through the manicured trees. She loves the smell of the grass being watered. The dark wash of the evening sky on the city lights. She doesn't want to think of the future. She can't.

30

The next morning, she starts painting figures, shapes of figures, like dead souls, cloaked in vestiges of religious apparel, heads bent in silence, emerging from the background of her dark landscapes.

Andrew stops by off the street. For a long time Angela hasn't seen him around. But now he's come back, to hang out, he says. If that's okay.

He sits on the couch, silent, sulking. Angela doesn't want him here. She doesn't want the smell of defeat and self-pity that comes off him like bad body odour. She feels bad she doesn't want him here.

I'm sorry Judy left you.

Why do things never work out how you want?

You want me to tell things are going to be okay.

I don't want anything.

She hates his silence, his paralysis of the will, the inertia, pulling her down, a weight on her. She wants him to go away.

I'm working, she says.

I won't bother you, he says.

Why doesn't she tell him to fuck off. She can't. She's a good person.

Nobody gives a give a shit about me.

I give a shit, she says.

You're just saying that, you don't mean it.

I want you to go, she says.

No problem, he says. If that's what you want.

It's what I want.

He gets up from the couch, slowly, moving against the inertia, the entropy in his body, his spirit. He goes to the door, stops, hesitating. I didn't mean to bother you, he says, guilting her out for rejecting him.

She knows what it's like to be rejected. To be left out. Not included. The hurt.

She runs after him. Don't be mad at me, she says.

I'm not, he says.

Yes you are, she says. I'll make some coffee.

He flops on the couch. Back in her good graces.

Instant okay?

Instant is good.

He says he's thinking of being a poet.

Nothing's stopping you.

Andrew gets up. I'm going, okay. I don't want to be where I'm not wanted.

Angela gets angry. It's never you, is it? You can blame Judy, the rest of us, society, so you don't have to do anything. Everybody else is supposed to make life better for you. Jesus, Andrew, grow up.

Andrew leaves. Angela lights a cigarette to calm her nerves. She goes back into her studio. She's feeling bad. Like she's done something wrong. She hasn't done anything wrong. It was him, dumping on her. Then why does she still feel bad?

He's going to tell other people she's a real bitch. They're going to think badly of her. She doesn't want people to think badly of her. Why not? Christine doesn't give a shit what people think of her. She gets away with blue murder and nobody says anything.

31

Angela backs off from her canvas. She can't break out of not colouring over the line taught in elementary school. She blocks in everything with colour. No mess. She can't end up with a mess. Everything in its place. A place and time for everything.

What if she paints and finds nothing? What if, in the end, her life is nothing.

Maybe she's playing. She's not really an artist. If she is, she's mediocre. She doesn't want to be mediocre. She should give up painting. Or writing. Who does she think she is?

Everybody so into themselves.

Even her. Being an artist. With her sublimated rage against the reality principle. Her required regression to primitivism. The gnosticism of the archetypal unconscious. The oneness of being. Beyond good and evil.

But there is evil. Damien is evil.

32

Cheryl shows up looking for her father Karl Hurst.

I'm sorry, Angela says. I don't mean to stare.

People can't help staring at the aesthetics of anorexia, Cheryl says.

Angela takes her suitcase and coat. Offers to make Cheryl something to eat.

Cheryl says she's not hungry. She doesn't drink coffee. Water would be okay.

Karl arrives. You've grown up.

Happens, she says.

She's beautiful, Angela says. Dark like you, Karl.

He says he thought her mother turned her against him.

She did. But I'm old enough to decide for myself. Are you going to marry Angela?

He's never asked, Angela says.

What if you said no? That would be the end of what we have, Karl says.

I have a job in the city, Cheryl says. Secretary in a law firm uptown.

There's not a lot of room but we can find you a space to sleep here until you find a place for yourself.

Thank you, Cheryl says. But I'm moving in with my boyfriend, Harold. He got a job in an auto body shop on the north end of the city. We've been girlfriend and boyfriend since grade five.

Karl asks about Cheryl's mother.

Bossy as ever. She got kicked out of Wendy's wedding rehearsal for trying to tell the priest what had to be done. And you, you're still full of anger. I saw your show. You're smearing paint on the canvas like it's shit. Like you're a victim raging against the injustices life gives us. Why are you so angry at the world/

How is your sister?

Wendy is Wendy. Life is a rose garden.

Dad didn't tell you his mother beat the crap out of him when he was a little kid. She killed what was inside him. She destroyed him. So he had to destroy everything, everybody around him, his revenge for what she did to him. It worked.

Look at me, Cheryl says. He found me, remember, dad. in an old warehouse in the old industrial scrapheap along the railway tracks. I had overdosed on your free love and drugs.

33

Angela greases her hair back. Paints on a moustache. She goes to the bar. So where does a man find any action in this town?

Phyllis breaks into her own self-absorbed dance, tight, controlled, with little movement, like she's holding the music down inside her, a crescendo building up, up, breaking. She lets loose, her head thrown back, dark hair wild, a grimace on her face, as she slices and stabs the air.

The music stops, her breathing hard, she laughs. She moves into the next dance, seductive temple slut dance.

34

Angel tells herself she has to stop feeling she has to prove herself. Stop pushing. She doesn't have to be a great painter, writer. For her they're therapy, getting her out of herself. If she gets published, good. A show, good. In the meantime, paint and writer. Keeps her going.

Maybe she should go back to church. Giving up on God has left with the void of being in a world that's running down, no hope, no purpose in life, nothing. The world doesn't forgive.

She can't forgive. Crap.

35

You were gone a long time, Karl says. Angela says she needed space.

Hungry?

Famished, she says.

Karl opens the fridge. We have tomatoes, cheese, mayonnaise. There's part of a loaf of bread.

You've never thought you had to look after me, have you?

We all want to be looked after, Karl says. Be told everything's going to be okay. That the world is going in end in a nuclear holocaust.

Do you know, back in school, if we were attacked to hide under our desks?

And if the Soviets attacked, Karl says, they'd flow over the flat land of Saskatchewan to the US.

I need a hug, Angela says.

Karl holds her in a big bear hug.

36

Angela comes from her bath in one of his work shirts, searches for her cigarettes, finds them behind the mattress. She pours herself a vodka and orange juice. She sits on the fire escape. The evening air is cool against the skin of her bare legs. Karl's working late. But she knows he's there in his studio. He exists. Which means she exists. They are more than mathematical constructs. Science can't explain what makes them human. Science can't explain how the world came into being. They have to have faith the answers will come. Angela can't explain. Maybe there are no answers. We all have to live not knowing.

She's having a hard time to stop building a wall so Karl can't get to her. He is so patient with her. But at some point, he is going to give up.

She pours herself another vodka.

37

How's mom and dad?

They're not going to change, says Christine.

And you and Eddie?

Fighting cats and dogs. Like always. Nothing's changed. My fault. But I can't stop myself. He says something, I have to contradict him. On trivial things. Nice day, it's a rotten day. I feel stupid if he doesn't agree with me. Sometimes I push his buttons until he yells. Then I've got him for yelling at me, his wife.

You're terrible.

I know. But I have to be top dog. ???

I don't know you anymore.

Funny, isn't it? You have a right to your opinions, but I don't.

You always thought you were smarter than me and the rest of us. You can't be wrong.

Show me where I'm wrong.

38

Christine has left home and came to Saskatoon where she has a job in a beauty parlour on Broad. Angela meets her off the train. Christine gets off with a cute soldier younger than her. She wants Angela to meet Freddy. He says he will see Christine but he has to get to the barracks.

You have to like men, Christine says. They're so easy, after one thing. All a woman has to do is string them along and she will get anything she wants. Free movies. Free dinners. Jewellery.

Until they have nothing left to give, Angela says.

Christine says she's thinking of cutting hair and becoming a broker.

39

Angela, browsing in a book store on Broad Street, bumps into Jason, literally. He says he's seen her landscapes. They're great. Angela's looking great. We'll have to get together sometime, he says. Then he's gone.

Angela stops in the cafe. The café is crowded with couples. She would like to do a series of paintings on couples. What made them couples? What holds them together? Wrapped in each other, themselves?

Angela looks at her landscape on the wall on the cafe wall.

They're good, says a man's voice behind her. An older man, in his fifties, grey, solid build, muscular in jeans and T-shirt, cropped brown-grey hair, a clarity in his brown eyes. She is attracted. There isn't the vacuous self-obsession she sees in other men. I'm sorry, he says. I haven't introduced myself. Father Zaval, he says.

You don't look like a priest, Angela says.

A monk, he says. From the monastery.

Why would you want to become a monk?

He is amused. Like you, he says, I am a rebel. A romantic. And I'd like to buy one of your paintings.

You're kidding, Angela says.

I wanted to be an artist once, he says.

But you have the power to forgive sins.

40

Angela turns from her canvas. She lights a cigarette and stands in the window of her studio. Below in the street, couples are out for a walk in the fresh, snow-melting, spring evening. She wishes she had their faith things will get better. It doesn't get better, kiddo. This is it. Get over it. Move on. Be happy.

Angela makes herself some instant coffee. Want some?

You should eat, Christine says.

I got a call from Hawkins, Angela says. He's in the city. He wants to see me. Take me out to dinner.

And you're going.

I liked him. He had a shoulder I could cry on.

She showers and dresses in her pants and top, pulls on her boots. In the restaurant, he orders a bottle of the house wine while they look at the menu. What does she suggest?

I'm having the salmon, she says. He says he'll have the salmon. He tells her he's not teaching school. He was fired. He'd been hitting the sauce. At the moment, he's selling life insurance. His daughter's in Montreal. She got a job on a television series. Script editor.

Angela asks about Petry.

Gone, he says. Miss Valdenson is principal.

And Gerald? Whatever has happened to him?

He came back from the oil fields and married Emily. They have a blonde baby girl, Barbara. He's a mechanic in her father's garage.

After Angela left, the school went down hill. He missed her. Their talks. Got him reading again. He's working on a book on the history of provincial politics.

Never too late, Angela says.

I still want to get you into bed, he says.

And ruin our friendship? Besides you wouldn't want to cross a line you can never cross back.

41

On the way to the community college art class where Angela agreed to teach for the semester, her old chevy stalls on the street. Now what? She's late. Sleet is falling on the street, freezing.

From the street corner phone booth, she calls Nathan. He says to hold tight, he'll bring his battery cables. Angela waits. Finally Nathan arrives and jump starts her car.

We will have to get together soon, he says.

Absolutely.

But they don't. Nathan has turned to drinking.

42

Christine says she can't make supper. Ferguson is taking me out.

Who's Ferguson?

A guy I met, Christine says.

One of these days, Angela says, I'm going to get a phone you've found in some back alley.

There's a story for you to write about, Christine says.

What happened to Brooks?

He wanted things his way.

43

Angela passes the synagogue where the neo-nazis have left their swastikas smeared in blood-red paint on the white walls still trying to cleanse the world of Jews. Angela is nauseated. She stops the car and gets out. She goes to the curb and vomits on the grass.

In her next life, she's not going to be an idealist, worrying about how the world ought to be. She's going to sell cosmetics and go on tax-evasion trips to Hawaii and come back suntanned and self-righteous. There is talk that non-whites in the country should get a quota of jobs where they merit the job or not. Blame the whites. Whites bad, Indians good. The myth of the Rousseau's noble savage, that is, the uncivilized man, un-corrupted by civilization. Which is bullshit because the tribes warred, tortured their enemies, took slaves, committed genocide.

Angela lights a cigarette to calm herself down.

You'll be called a racist, Christine says.

I have to be a racist or the anti-racists can't be anti-racist.

They argue, based on their feelings, their so-called compassion for the underdog, Bart says, their hatred of those that get ahead in life by hard work, systemic racism exists in the country's institutions. They don't wanna work, they live off welfare, writers and artists, who know people, live off the government tit.

From what I hear, Jason says, it's reality. I took a workshop on getting ahead. We were told the arts are ninety per cent brown-nosing.

Which I'm not good at, Angela says. Growing up, we were told not to blow your own horn.

It's who you know, Jason says. And you have to be a leftist because the arts are run by the left.

I'd rather paint and write what I want, Angela says. Or what's the point?

What's the point if your paintings are stacked in your studio and your writing's in a drawer?

I put a painting in the Sherman Gallery, Angela says. It didn't make it into the show. They never even took off the wrapping.

Weren't artists told, Jason says, what to paint?

Wasn't there a guy, Bart says, an Italian, who advocated getting control of cultural institutions, education, media, the arts, to move the politics to the left. The utopia.

The so-called utopia when the left legislate censorship, imprison those who don't go along with the party line.

You'd think, Angela says, looking at the gulags in the Soviet Union, communism would be dead.

Has nothing to do with reason, Bart says, ideology is based of feeling, on wanting to feel you're important, you're somebody in the world.

Used to be the proletariat, Jason says, who were oppressed by the bourgeoisie. Stalin saw that the bourgeoisie were tried in kangaroo courts and then shot, buried in mass graves. Or sent to gulags in the Siberia where they died from malnutrition and the freezing cold.

Listen to you, Christine says to Angela.

Like the KGB, Bart says, you must have neighbours who rat out the racists.

We don't have gulags in this country, Christine says.

Not yet.

I didn't know you were such a right-wing wingnut, Christine says to Angela.

You bleeding hearts don't have an argument, so you put down those who don't agree with you. We're called racists to shut us up.

I don't know if I want you for a sister.

I thought we lived in a country where the individual has a right to think and say what they want. Guess not.

Jason says he took a workshop on getting ahead. We were told the arts are ninety per cent brown-nosing.

Which I'm not good at, Angela says. Growing up, we were told not to blow your own horn.

I'd rather paint and write what I want. Jason says. Or what's the point?

Maybe, Bart says, we have to become leftists. Like what's the point if your paintings are stacked in your studio and your writing is in a drawer?

44

Christine goes with Angela to the group show. She's not impressed with Karl's splatterings. And this, she says. She looks at the name. Eddie Bloomfield.

He's a minimalist, Angela says.

Anal retentive, Christine says. You should think of doing an installation out of used Tampax stuffed into semen-soaked condoms dropped floating in condoms. That'd be radical.

They are approached by Beatrice who curated the show.

What do they think of the show?

Before they can answer, Beatrice scoots off and disappears in the crowd.

Christine goes to the wine table. She brings back a glass of wine for Angela, who is left standing like a wallflower. She sees Karl in the avant garde coterie surrounding Beatrice. It's his night.

A Harold Hutt introduces himself to Angela. He's a short, thick, bearded man, sculptor and self-professed primitive. I'm in love with you, he says.

You are very drunk, Angela says.

That too, he says. What did you say your name was?

I didn't.

An aging poet hovers beside Beatrice. He tells her it is so good to see her.

Funny, she says, how we end up where we started.

Expensive to live in Toronto.

Why I never left here.

We must get together.

Soon, she says, beelining across the room. You decided to show up, she says. Sergie's an up-and-coming pop artist who loves Warhol's Brillo box.

I did, he says.

I love the pieces you're making.

I'm trying.

Don't be modest, Beatrice says. We have too much modesty. Modesty begets mediocrity. When artists and poets, by definition, are egotistical hustlers. Besides, she says, there's too much nauseating narcissism coming out of today's incestuous poetry scene. When we need poetry that's gritty, hard-edged, brutally honest. Like Sergie's, she says.

Sergie sucks on his beer while listening to Karl going on about abstraction expressionism which gets us out of the brutal reality of the war, giving us space to meditate in peace. A chick is engrossed with the words coming out of his mouth.

Methinks the lady's going to get fucked, Christine says.

Angela says she is leaving.

Christine says she will find her own way back. The guy from the Sundog Theatre can't keep his eyes off her.

His name is Brooks, Angela says.

Christine goes up to Brooks. I want to get to know you, she says.

We can't know the other, he says.

I know you want to get to know me, she says.

Your place or mine?

45

Angela doesn't get into the city art show. Neither does Michal. Fuck it, he says. Angela stops off at Tony's Bar where she asks for a rum and coke, dark. Slow night, she says. It's early, Tony says. You okay?

Don't ask, Angela says.

One of those days, he says.

Angela likes Tony. A big man, late forties, balding, walrus moustache, thick neck like a bull, ex football player. According to Tony, the season isn't looking good. To make the playoffs, the Roughriders have to win against the Lions. Tony isn't betting.

His peroxide blonde, over-aged cheerleader wife comes down from the living quarters above the bar. She goes behind the bar and pours herself a stiff drink. She climbs back up the stairs, sah-shaying her big ass.

Tony busies himself wiping down the bar. The waitress brings Angela an ashtray.

Tony's in love with you, y'know, she says.

Tony loves the whole world, Angela says.

Angela downs her drink and leaves. In the street she is accosted by a gang of hoodlums. They want her purse, which grabbed out of her hands.

I bet you've got nice tits, says the leader, ripping open her coat and clawing at the buttons on her blouse, exposing her small breasts. Angela covers herself. What kind of cowards are you, you'd attack a woman?

Bitch, the leader snarls.

Yeah, right. This coming from a loser.

You think I'm a loser?

So what are you going to do? Beat up, a woman to prove you're a man?

Let's go, says his sidekick.

46

Christine says she hates hospitals. She hates the smell of ether and the disinfectants they wash the floors with. She hates the labyrinth of hallways and closed doors. A bad dream she can't get out of.

I didn't think you'd come, Angela says.

What are you doing here?

I wanted to kill myself, Angela says.

Why?

I don't want to live any more?

But you're here.

I know, but I don't know how much longer I can drag myself through days of depression.

You have to, Christine says. You can't be so selfish as to off yourself. What about me? I need you. You're the only person in the whole world I can trust with my secrets.

It's the schizophrenia.

You're not schizophrenic, Christine says.

I hear voices.

What voices?

They tell me nobody gives a shit about me, I should kill myself.

They're wrong, Christine says. I give a shit.

I live in my own reality.

We all live in our own reality.

We're all schizophrenic.

I'm not a good person, Angela says.

Who is?

I'm sorry, Angela says.

Aren't there pills that can help you with depression?

I don't like taking pills.

You're gonna have to, aren't you? And get on with your life.

What life?

Your art. Christine says.

Are you happy?

No, I'm not happy, Christine says. I've made a mess of my life.

You should do something, Angela says.

Like what? I'm not talented like you, Christine says.

You like to be with people.

So I should get a job as a TV. hostess on some game show. Not gonna happen.

You could set up your own beauty parlour. You're good at it.

Christine sits on the edge of the bed. She brushes the hair out of Angela's eyes. You can't go on like this, Christine says.

Think I want to?

Tell me who he was, says Christine. I'll kill him.

He's not worth going to prison.

I'm not going to jail. I'm going to go back, invite him to my hotel room, pour him wine, laugh at him fucking me, and after, serve him hors d'oeuvres laced with salmonella, which will be blamed on the hotel.

You've watched too many movies.

You could write a screenplay how a woman gets rid of abusive men so they can't continue hurting women.

I shouldn't have agreed to go see his studio. But I was drunk.

Listen, kiddo. Wasn't your fault. Stop blaming yourself.

But I feel so dirty.

Christine puts her arms around her. You have to stop being so hard on yourself.

I feel like I've done something wrong, I'm going to die and go to hell. Even God can't forgive me.

Don't talk to me about God, Christine says. God let it happen.

Why me?

I don't know why, Christine says. All I know is that you can't change what happened. What you should've, should've not done. You're just torturing yourself. I know he took away your trust in people, in the world. It could happen again. But you can't live that way. You have to trust yourself it won't happen again. Look, you haven't even combed your hair.

Nobody's going to want to marry me, Angela says.

Jason wanted to.

Jason wanted to be a saint and save me.

You have to save yourself.

I'm having trouble falling asleep. And I can't stop eating. I'm going to be fat as a pig.

Christine studies her reflection in the windowpane against the night. Wasn't supposed to be like this, she says. You being in here. Little Miss Muffett. She buttons her coat.

Do you have to go?

I'll see you tomorrow, okay?

Why do we lie to each other?

Because the truth gets us into trouble, Christine says. And why haven't you left Karl?

47

Angela is released from St Paul's. A deadbeat approaches her. The end of the world is near, he says. Angela's out of cigarettes, so she crosses the street to the convenience store. A gaggle of kids, twelve-fourteen year-olds, crowd the entrance to the convenience store. They let Angela through. She goes in and buys a pack of cigarettes. Comes out.

Give us a cigarette, says one of the older boys. Angela tries to ignore him, but she's surrounded with surly faces.

Ya heard Yak. Give us a cigarette.

What are you going to do? Beat me up on the street?

Listen, lady, nobody will give a shit. They'll go right by.

Yak grabs at her purse. A car stops. Getting out is a middle-aged woman. What the fuck?

She comes at the them waving her medal cane. Yak and his thugs hightail it to the back alley.

You okay?

You didn't have to, Angela says.

What? And let these little bastards get away with beating up a woman, I don't think so.

Angel lights a cigarette. Thank you, she says.

Do you need a ride?

I don't think they're coming back.

I wish they'd stayed around and I could've bashed a few of them, they can attack a woman.

Maybe I should get a medal cane, Angela says.

Wouldn't be a bad idea.

48

Christine finishes her scotch. Says she would love to stay and yuk with Nathan but she has to run. Maybe they can be friends. Someday he'll run into the right woman. A man should fall in love at least once in his life, it's what makes the world go round. Can't be in love and not be optimistic about the future.

Except there is no future in love, Nathan says.

Don't. Self-pity doesn't look good on you.

I'm not looking for you to fall in love with me. All I want is to sleep with you.

Yeah, Christine says. And fall in love with me. No thanks. But you never know. I might change my mind.

There is hope.

There is always hope. But a woman goes to bed with a man, he starts to think he owns her. They will end up fighting. He will hate her. She does not want him to hate her.

She does not want to make a commitment, he says.

I really do have to run, she says. Que sera, sera.

She files through the crowded tables. She smiles at the guy near the door. He smiles back. She stops and talks to him. She writes down her phone number and gives it to him.

49

Been a long day, Brooks says. I'm wiped. I can't get Sara to reach down into her character. What does her character want? What is she willing to do to get what she's wants?

What we all want, Angela says. To be seen, recognized. Told we're important in this world.

Brooks complains about Maurice. From the start of rehearsals, Maurice has been a pain in the ass, delivering what is required. Says he's conserving his creative energy.

Brooks says he's hungry. Angela goes with him across the street to Wong's Kitchen where they join Sara, who is ordering won-ton. Says she's thinking of going to Toronto. Maybe something big will happen for her.

You should go, Brooks says. You're young.

Sara wants to know what he thinks of Beatrice and John.

They're the beautiful people, Angela says. Why?

John wants to be my friend.

I'm friends with John, Angela says. He's a good man.

But why does he want to be my friend?

Get away from Beatrice a bit.

I would like to come unto you, Brooks says.

But you won't, Sara says.

Angela orders won-ton.

I want to go to Toronto, Sara says, but I'm worried about leaving my sister. She didn't know until after they were married, she would have to walk on egg shells. She leaves him and goes back home. But after a day, she wants him to come and pick her up. Like a yo-yo. She doesn't see it's dragging her down. It's like she doesn't want a life. She can blame him she doesn't do anything with her life. I'm sorry. You guys don't want to hear about my problems. Jesus, she's cutting herself. I try telling her and she gets on my case. What makes me think I'm so perfect?

She doesn't want help.

I can't help worrying about her. She stares down at her soup. She looks so young and vulnerable in her boyish haircut. Like I'm one to talk, she says. I have a knack for going for the bad boys. I'm going to make them love me. Pretty stupid. I have to simplify my life. Maybe I should go back to my hometown.

With their small-town mindedness, Angela says. The optimistic certainty of their cliché lives. Everything is the way it's suppose to be. Indoor plumbing, now electricity, television, Hockey Night in Canada. Artificial ice in the curling rink. Everything uncomplicated.

Old friends who have moved away, Sara says. Jordan. Mike. Mildred. Who married Keith Chowski. He took over his old man's tire shop. Mildred, from what I hear, strayed from the path of righteousness. Came back. For the sake of the children, community, chastised, repentant. The wages of sin.

Stafford comes in. You look like shit, he says to Brooks. He sits down at their table. You're not looking after yourself.

Brooks buys him a cup of coffee.

I hear you're going back to Toronto, Angela says.

Nothing here for me, he says.

50

John climbs up to Angela's studio. He is puffing from the climb. He wants to let her know everything's been finalized for her show opening. Angela scrounges for her cigarettes. She's nervous. She doesn't have to be, he says. Everything's been taken care of. He will pick her up later, he says. Try to be ready.

For a long time, Angela sits on the fire escape. The pavement is wet from the cold drizzle. A premonition. She hopes not.

For supper, she makes a hamburger for herself, which she washes down with a glass of wine. Showers and gets dressed.

John is back for her. He lights up a cigarette in the back of the taxi and waits, tolerantly. Angela finally comes down. Says for him to go, she will catch up to him. I don't know how I'm going to make it through this evening. These past few days finishing up her paintings have been draining.

I'm sure the show is going to be a success, John says.

We can hope.

51

Angela looks in her mailbox. Bills. No letter. In the kitchenette, she makes herself a cup of instant coffee. She sits down at the table with the coffee and smokes a cigarette. Stafford said he would write. He's not going to write. The bugger.

She finishes the cigarette and goes up to the bedroom where she undresses and crawls into a hot bath and soaks. Drying herself, she dresses in pants and work shirt. Her hair is still wet. She sits down on the bed and smokes another cigarette. She's smoking too much. She blow-dries her hair, which falls flat. She has to do something with her hair. Maybe a perm. She hates perms.

She packs her paints, easel, and a couple of small canvases and hikes down to the riverbank where, in the sun, she sets up to paint the river and the blue prairie sky. She sits on her stool and lights a cigarette. Here, on the riverbank, thousands of years ago, a young girl came down to the river to get over a broken heart. She is watched by an old crow in the trees behind her, cawing when wolves showed up, stalking her. The old crow protects her from the evil spirits that have possessed the wolves.

Back in her studio, Angela paints a wolf howling against the full moon in the dead of night.

52

John gathers a crowd around the podium where he gives a speech. Angela, he says, in her paintings, explores the theme of alienation, the negative space that separates us, that makes us into shadows of our self. She is asking us what has happened, what's gone wrong? What have we lost? What will bring us back together? She asks these questions. It's up to us to find the answers, he says.

There is the polite clapping of hands. Then the audience breaks up into cliques.

John approaches Angela. She promised she wouldn't be late.

Angela apologizes. She lost track of the time.

A good crowd, John says.

Beatrice comes over with a male friend. You should be pleased with yourself, she says to Angela. She turns to John. Why don't you see if you can find us something to drink? Angela here is awfully thirsty, aren't you, darling?

Yes, awfully, says Angela.

John asks what Beatrice will have.

I should think a bit of white wine would be nice.

Angela says she will have white wine.

You haven't met Andrew Crandell. He came from Britain to teach art. Andrew, this is Angela.

You practice art?

Drips and drabs, he says. Life seems to take over.

Beatrice surveys the crowd. These affairs are so awfully anti-climatic, don't you think? Such a letdown afterwards. You look bored, dear. But then artists are easily bored, aren't they? They easily get tired of things, of everybody. They want to get on with new things, new beginnings. A special contempt for the old. The mundane. It's why they're artists and we're not. We get used to the way things are in our drip-and-drab life.

Crandell wants to go.

Yes, of course, dear, says Beatrice. What was I saying? Yes. I remember. I was going to say the artist is the lover. It is through his art we find wholeness, like the lover, who completes us. Makes our world beautiful, don't you think? What is needed is the polymorphous perversity of the artist.

John rescues Angela, driving her home. The poor bugger's in love with her.

53

Angela drags herself out of bed. Puts coffee on. Showers. Gets dressed. Smokes a cigarette, looking at a poem she'd written. Butts her cigarette in the ashtray and finishes her coffee. She puts on her winter coat and, out the door, she climbs down to the street. She climbs back up and goes in to make sure the cigarette butt is out. It won't burn down the rooming house. She goes out and locks the door. Unlocks the door and goes back in. The cigarette butt is out. She goes out and locks the door, climbing down to the street. She climbs back to make sure the door is locked. It's locked. She heads back down the stairs, forcing herself not to back up to check she'd locked the door. Maybe she should check she'd shut off the stove. No.

54

Angela stops in the Nova Art Gallery. A Terry Galvin is having a show of prairie landscapes. Angela went to high school with a Terry Galvin. He was in the same grade. They were the best of friends. But, after high school, they went their different ways, he, at art school in Calgary, she staying here in Saskatchewan.

She looks at the art statement on the wall.

It's me, a voice says. Angela turns around. There he is, good-looking as ever. His big smile. You haven't changed, she says.

I hope I have, he says. Or I'd still be the dork borrowing your French homework to copy.

You were never a dork, she says.

What have you been doing since high school?

Got my arts degree. Went teaching. Come here, taking part time jobs so I could paint.

I went the art school in Calgary, he says. Went back home to the Queen City. Got married. Sharon got a job in St Paul's. I've been teaching school. And painting as much as I find time.

Your realism captures the mood of the prairie frozen in time. A day in the sun. Just you and the prairie grass, the brown hills against the blue sky. I love being in your prairie.

You must invite me to your studio, he says.

Pretty much a mess right now, she says. My life's pretty much a mess right now.

You married?

I should've married my best friend in high school. Doesn't take long for the passion to die out. Don't be a stranger, she says, leaving the gallery. Down the street, she stops in a bar for a drink. She has to make changes in her life. She can't keep going on like this. If only she could feel better. Be happy. Maybe she should consider shock treatment. It is said to work. But look what it did for Michal. But she has to do something.

She sits by the business man at the counter. Can I buy you another drink?

A rum and coke? Knock yourself out.

She orders two rum and cokes. What's a guy like you doing in a place like this?

I could ask you the same question.

I want to get laid, Angela says.

Maybe I could oblige you, he says. I have a room in this hotel.

I have to finish my drink. You have a name?

Callum. You?

Angeline.

Glad to meet you, Angeline.

She sips on her rum and coke.

He asks what she does when she's not a home.

I'm an artist.

Always a good hobby.

It's not a hobby. Art can change the world.

I like the world the way it is, he says. The good, the bad and the ugly.

She follows him up to his hotel room where she sits on the edge of the bed while he pours the two of them a Caribou Crossing whisky.

You're married?

Does that matter?

Not to me.

He takes off his suit jacket and loosens his tie. He is a good-looking man with a full head of hair, square jaw and a genuine smile. I have to tell you, he says, I've never done this before. In fact, I don't know if I can.

Pour me another whisky, Angela says.

55

Angela locks the door, Sinks into the big chair. A heaviness comes over her. She struggles to get up, going to the bathroom. Gets off the toilet and runs a hot bath. She sinks into the hot water and soaks. Release the stress that grips her brain. Like her brain is going to explode.

She soaps her body. She's putting on weight. Opening her legs, she scrubs her vagina.

Angela dries herself. In the mirror, she looks pale, drawn. There are dark circles under her

eyes. Stress from trying to survive. Nobody's buying her portraits of lost souls that haunt the Queen's Hotel.

She dresses and warms up a can soup for supper. She stands at the window. The sun is setting on the city. Down on the street, an old man yanks on the binder twine, dragging his mongrel dog off the sidewalk into the street, which he crosses. Angela wants to go down and yank him.

She eats her hot soup, putting the dirty dishes into the sink and washes them in hot water and dish detergent, leaving the clean dishes to dry on a tea towel spread out on the kitchen counter.

She leaves her rooms to buy cigarettes and the newspaper.

56

In her apartment, Angela throws the poetry book on the coffee table, takes off her coat and puts on some classical music. She runs hot water into her tub while she finds some candles, which she lights and puts on the edge of the tub. She undresses and sinks into the oiled water. She shouldn't have gone and visited her mother. Her voice a monologue of complaints.

You never tell me what's going on in your life, her mother said.

You've never want to know.

Of course, I've want to know.

I had a show last month.

Why don't you come back home? You should be getting married. Having children.

I have my own life.

I didn't bring you up to be selfish.

I'm sorry you're not happy, mom. But it's not my fault you're not happy. I can't make you happy. You have to make yourself happy.

We weren't put on earth to be happy.

What did the doctor say?

What do they know?

Did you go see the doctor?

There's nothing wrong with me, he mother said.

I love your flowers, Angela said.

hey didn't grow like they should, her mother said. They didn't get enough light. There's no light in here.

How's grandmother?

She's going to be the death of me.

What happened, mom? Why has it come to this?

Come to what?

You hiding yourself in the house.

I do no such thing.

It's like you've given up on yourself, on life.

You're young, says her mother. You don't know everything. You'll get old. Maybe then you won't be so quick to judge.

Your cake is good, mom.

Angela should get out of the tub. She's out of cigarettes.

57

Angela smokes a cigarette in her studio. Nothing's coming. She goes back to bed. She's going to be self-indulgent. She listens to the bird outside the window. It makes the sound leitto. Means summer is coming.

She gets up and goes down to the kitchenette where she makes herself a cup of coffee, takes the coffee to the couch, lights up a cigarette and, absentmindedly, picks up a book of short stories, starts reading, curled up on the couch with her coffee and cigarette and loneliness. ???

"He behind, his cock ramming into her as he fucks her like a fucking machine turned on high. Then, shoving his cock to the hilt, he comes.

He rolls off her and lies on the bed, sweating. Hot in here, he says.

She gets up and goes to the washroom where she showers. She comes back and he, his head propped up by pillows on the bed, is smoking a cigarette. Will I see you again?

58

Christine comes over. She models her new yellow sundress. Maybe something good will happen.

A yellow dress and pink hat? Angela says.

Too much yellow, you think?

I wish I could be you, Angela says.

You wouldn't want to be me, says Christine. I'm a real she-bitch, remember.

Your high octane energy, Angela says.

59

Angela buries herself, her life, in her studio, where she works. An obsession. A good obsession. She's making progress. She's learning more about colour. Simplifying colour and form. Essence. What is the essence?

Is there any essence?

Maybe there's nothing behind things. There are no explanations. She's left with the unknown. Left with paint and canvas. Painting. The act of painting. A performance. All there is.

She goes to a poetry reading with Ellis. Christine doesn't want to go. She hates poetry readings. They're boring. Worse than being in church, she says.

After the reading, Ellis introduces Angela to Garner.

She says she read his book of poems. They're good.

Gritty. Hard-edged. A poet to watch, Garner says.

Don't make fun of me, Angela says.

I'm sorry.

If you're really and truly, cross your heart and promise to die sorry, you can buy me a coffee.

The coffee shop is deserted. They take a table in the corner. Over the table on the wall is a mural of a purple mountain and blue river.

Garner gets the coffee. She'll be here when he gets back?

She'll be here.

Forever?

Forever is a very long time, she says.

Christine hears Angela is spending time with a poet. Angela didn't tell her.

Christine doesn't have to know everything.

Yes, I do, Christine says. Where is he? When do I get to meet him?

60

Angela experiments with flowers and colour. So much to learn. Hue. Value. Complementary colours. Harmony. Dominance balanced against the subordinated parts. If not, it ends in a cluttered mess. She has to get to her appointment with the psychiatrist.

61

Christine shows up in sunglasses. She takes them off. She has to stop hooking up with the wrong guys.

So why doesn't she go back to her husband?

Christine gags.

What am I going to do with you?

Nothing you can do, says Christine. You heard from Garner?

Angela tells Christine of her dream. A large oval-shaped birdcage, Angela says. I'm trying to feed the baby birds. An old Chinese man comes into the dream. He shows me how to feed the birds.

That afternoon, Angela says, in the street, an old Chinese man stops her. He has a birdcage. Angela doesn't have money on her.

She should've written him a cheque, she says.

Christine says she dreamt she fell into a cistern. A man stands up top. She yells for him to help her. He walks away. Night comes.

62

Beatrice comes up to Angela's studio. She wants Angela to stay away from her husband.

Who?

You know who. John is a weak man. But he's all she has.

Angela hasn't seen him. Beatrice doesn't believe her. Angela's already ruined Stafford's marriage.

Angela is taking pictures of herself with the self-timer on the camera. A succession of pictures. Different poses, different facial expressions, different poses in the nude. She wants to move more and more to abstraction in her paintings.

She sprawls out on her back, her arms outstretched like the crucifix. She covers herself, ashamed, she shouldn't be, is.

Beatrice finds herself a chair and sits. She is a large, solid woman. From peasant stock.

She lights a cigarette. She offers Angela a cigarette. Angela gets up and takes the offered cigarette. She lets Beatrice light it for her and, still nude, sits on the floor.

Beatrice says she thinks she understands what Angela is doing. Something to do with how we're seen, want to be seen, she says. What image we want to project.

What image people project on us, says Angela.

We have to forgive them, Beatrice says. Forgive ourselves. She smells of body odour and outrage. She makes a pot of tea from the chamomile she has in her purse. We think we have to be perfect or people won't like us. We give them too much say in our lives. She ended up carrying that man on her back. She carried the weight. Her own fault. She was going to build him into something. She laughs. She picked a man who let her control him. She got mad at him and he pulled that sloppy grin on her. She could knock his head off.

She misses the old bugger. Horribly.

But she's not taking him back. He doesn't love her. He doesn't have it in him. Still the little boy. Doesn't want to grow up.

She should get going. Do you like your tea stronger? I have to confess, she says. I was wrong about you, Angela. Wrong about a lot of things. I thought things worked out for the best. She laughs. I don't make a good martyr, do I?

Why are you telling me? Because, Beatrice says, you've been screwing around with my husband. I came to thank you. You freed me. I finally don't have to care anymore what happens to him.

63

Angela tries painting. Nothing's coming. She gives up, locks up her studio and descends to the street. She goes to a hairstylist. She says she wants to change her image.

How about a bob?

With my kinky hair?

Well lets go with the kinks and see what we get.

Angela lets her hair get cut. She doesn't like the cut. She never likes the cut.

She stops in an outdoor cafe. Christine shows up. She likes cafes, They're public places where everything is arranged for her. She doesn't have to do anything.

You look anorexic, Angela says. I've never understood the obsession with how we looked. The more the anxiety, self-doubts, self-loathing, the heavier the makeup. It's like women who have never outgrown the natural narcissism of the adorable child.

You're worried about my obsessions and I'm worried that you're becoming a slut, Christine says.

Me?

I thought you didn't want to be me.

I've always wanted to be like you. You're never uptight.

Me? I'm always anxious people won't like me.

Men like you.

I'm nothing but a prop for them to fuck.

Why can't we be ourselves? You the beautiful blonde bombshell. And me?

You're beautiful.

Not like you.

You don't have to be me. In fact, you wouldn't want to be me. I don't have the brains you have.

You have brains.

I didn't get the grades you did.

I didn't skip school.

Why you never had friends.

I had my books.

Which has made you questioning everything.

It's called skepticism.

The government never does anything right.

We need a new flag because Quebec doesn't want the union jack. They get what they want. To hell with the rest of Canada. Especially us in the colonies here in the west.

I've been with John for six months, Christine says.

Which is a record, Angela says.

I was with Eddie for two years, Christine says.

Who left you because he couldn't take you running around on him.

I've only got one life and I'm gonna live my life. What about you? You're getting a reputation.

I'm no angel.

Who says you have to be an angel?

Men can say all they want but, if you want to be loved and not just fucked, you have to be an angel.

Love? Christ. They tell you they love you but all they want is to get you into bed. Then they get tired of you and start looking around.

You and I have never been loved, Angela says. Father was in his own world. And mother...

Oh, yeah, mother. Religious mother. Thou shalt not.

You did anyway.

What about you? You hid in your room.

Have you ever seen this photograph?

That's our grandfather when he was young, Angela says.

Handsome dude with that blond hair and blue eyes, Christine says.

Grandma accused him of being in love with the widow across the back alley. A German woman. It was the time, during the first war, Germans were sent to internment camps.

I remember grandma saying the widow hid her shapely body under her winter coat. Angela says. But grandpa would have seen her hanging clothes on the clothes line, her dress pressed to her body by the summer winds.

Nobody can help who they fall in love with, Christine says.

He swore he never cheated on grandma.

Doesn't mean he didn't want to.

I believed him, Angela says, that he never cheated on grandma.

We know, Christine says, that he helped her out by chopping wood and carrying water from the town pump. So he did go in the house. The gossip started. But then people want to think the worst. Gloating that it's not them. They're good and decent people.

Her name, Angela says, was Katja Meier. She was the author of the novel, The Last Chapter, translated into English, in which the daughter of a noble family runs off with an older man to the big city. He soon grows tired of her and she finds herself living on the streets. According to the review, the novel was written in cold, objective, dispassionate prose, which, ironically, makes the reader feel the strength in the girl to survive having to prostitute herself until she had the money to buy a place to live in the poor parts of the city from which she wrote newspaper articles on what was really happening in the underbelly of their great city.

Wish I had the guts, Christine says. But then I'm not the writer.

64

Angela stops in the Zodiac. An aging poet is on the small stage beating a boran and chanting. He stops and explains to the small crowd sitting in the darkness that he is trying to get to the subconscious where words don't exist. Words have lost their meaning, he says. He beats the drum.

Angela finds a table in the back corner. A tall, thin man, handsome in long hair and grey beard, dressed in a sort of a monk robe, like one of the disciples, brings her a coffee. You're new here, he says. His name is John.

The poet finishes his act. He takes his boran off stage and sits with a circle of young friends. They are pleased with his performance. A woman, in her fifties, mounts the stage with an acoustic guitar. She is still beautiful, a full-busted woman, a glimpse of the her nipples pushing against her laced, chiffon blouse. She takes the microphone. Says her name is Beatrice. She is going to sing a song she wrote. A hymn really. A celebration of the creator. Her song is titled, We Are One.

You're Angela, says John. We're heard good things about you from Ellis. He says you're an artist.

Trying to be, Angela says.

We're all trying to be, says John.

65

Eddie is looking for Christine.

Angela hasn't seen her.

He's lost her, hasn't he?

You never had her, Angela says.

I know I should forget about her, he says. But I can't. It's like I want to be pissed on.

She isn't pissing on you, Angela says.

I know, he says. She's being herself.

He apologizes for coming. Don't tell Christine I was here, he says.

66

She falls in the snow. The snow covers her. She breathes through a hole in the snow. A man is standing over her. Her father. He gets on a train. The train pulls out onto the prairie. She's left on the station platform, his wool socks she was to give him in her hands. She watches as the train climbs into the distant hills.

She returns to the house. People come and gather round the dining room table. She doesn't know who the people are. She gets up from the table and goes upstairs. She undresses and, naked in the yellow light from the light-bulb that hangs from the ceiling, she stands at the window. In the moonlight, there is a field of blossoms. We can't leave, she says, turning to the man on the bed. She can't see who it is. The car has made tracks in the flowers. She starts singing. Sings and sings. She coughs from a sore throat. In the yard, Jason is waiting for her. Everyone says she's to go back to him. I don t want to, she says.

Then she is sitting on the couch downstairs. Jason comes and sits beside her. There are tubes in her nose. I worry about you, he says. He gets up. He is reading her poetry. Afterwards he comes up to her. He wants her to come back. She won't. He gets mad and stomps out of the house in rubber boots. He falls off the pier into the ocean. In the bright sunlight the water is very blue. The ferryboat looks very beautiful on the blue water. She is seated in a small bare room. In the corner, a man masturbates. She can't see his face. He is grinning because he knows she sees him, that she is watching. Christine is sleeping on the floor. Angela doesn't want to wake her. She stands in the doorway and looks down the grass slope down to the blue, blue water of the ocean. Jason comes with another woman. The woman stays in the hallway. She is lying on her side, her head propped up on her elbow. There is the rise of her hips. Jason comes into the small bare room and kisses Angela. He leaves. There is nothing I can do but wait until the sixteenth, she says. A strange man and her are on the bed talking. Outside in the night, a strong wind blows against the wall of the house. Our love doesn't feel real, she says. There is a gathering of people on the hillside. She can't find him in the crowd. An old man is standing beside his truck. She recognizes him. The old poet. She asks if he wants to spend some time with her? He says yes, climbing the grassed slope to the sea. She follows, carrying a blanket.

It is early morning. The sun is bright on the frozen hills across the lake. The lake is covered with snow. You're not going to stay, are you? You came to visit. You're not real. They are driving on a dirt road. The motor conks out. They are stranded in the middle of nowhere. A young man in a brown suit stops to help them. His young wife is wearing a yellow-brown dress. Angela is wearing the same dress but with more red in it, more earth tones. They go into the house. It is abandoned. They make coffee to thank the young man and his young wife. The door to the dining room is ajar. Inside is a crowd of people. A banquet. On the table are two large turkeys, a plain, roasted turkey and a butterball turkey. Angela says there is too much food. Where is Mr. Cox? She goes to find him upstairs. There is a younger woman below on the terrace. She is wearing a black dress and black hat with a white ruffle down the side. The young woman swings a golf club, hits the ball, with a flip of her hip, looks up at everybody and smiles, flippantly. Nobody knows who the young woman is. Angela wants to be the young woman. The children want to go out in the yard to play. But there is weed killer in the yard so they have to stay in the house. Angela goes into the yard and clears the snow so the children can play in the yard. There is a hollow in the snow like an igloo where the children can play. But she doesn't want the children to play in the igloo. It might fall and smother them. She is waiting in the house for her brother Arthur to come. He comes and pours a beautiful liquid for her. There are pearls in the liquid. Outside the window, a fire is burning. Angela gets up from the table and climbs the stairs. She undresses and, naked in the yellow electric light, she stands at the window. In the moonlight there is a field of violet blossoms. Jason has come to the house. He doesn't look well. He looks emasculated. Simone enters with a poet. Beautiful, blasphemous Simone. The dark angel. Her dark lined eyes. Black lipstick. The provocative shock of slick black hair. The contempt.

Angela goes to the kitchen. She helps herself to the leftover hors d'oeuvres. A glass of wine. She goes into the backyard. It is dark. The night closing in.

Simone is telling Jason she'll fuck the poet if she feels like it. Jason pulls out a toy gun. He points the gun at Simone. He shoots her through her black heart. She laughs.

Angela sits on her suitcase and waits by the road. A big white convertible drives up and stops. It is Arthur with that stupid grin on his face. He asks if she wants to go with him.

Arthur is dead, Christine says.

Angela goes up to her digs. She sits on the edge of the bed. A rattlesnake slithers up from inside her. It is choking her to death. She reaches inside and pulls it out, biting off it's head.

67

In her dream, it's night, dark, no moon. She is going down to the water. The water is black. She strips naked and wades into the water. She is afraid of the water. Even as a child she had been afraid. But she keeps going. Slowly. She lets the dark water rise up her legs, thighs, her waist, washing up over her breasts. Her feet sinking into the mud. The primeval ooze.

She wakes up before she sinks too far into the ooze. The primeval ooze. Where she came from. We all came from, crawling out on to the land, growing scrawling frog legs. We got up on our legs. For good and evil.

On the radio, she catches Martin Luther King's speech: "I have a dream that my four little children will one day live in a nation where they will not be judged by the colour of their skin but by the content of their character."

68

In the coffee shop, Angela runs into Bart Finley, the playwright whose play she went to see in the basement of the neighbourhood church. In the play, a fourteen year old takes a gun in the parking lot and shoots dead a young woman pushing a baby carriage. A senseless act of violence.

Eddie says he's met somebody, Eddie says, an older woman, a poet. Her name is Chloe Zukas. She's different, makes up her own rules. She likes putting on heavy makeup, dressing up in rhinestone dresses with dangling earrings and loads of rings on her fingers. She has a bit of a big nose. But she's great. In her poetry, she says what she feels has to be said. Being there's talk of shutting down the mental institutions in the province, Chloe writes to the newspaper that it's stupid to shut down the mental institutions, putting the mentally ill on the streets where they can't look after themselves.

Know what Chloe told me? She was a book festival, says Eddie, and got drunk and let a poet fuck her and now he wants more than a fuck from her. She's trying to get rid of him.

So why are you with her?

I'm not.

Good. More time to write plays.

69

Angela carries the two bags of groceries up the stairs to her rooms, puts the coffee on, the groceries away and changes into her paint clothes and, with a cup of coffee and cigarette, looks at the canvas on the easel. With turpentine, she thins her cadmium yellow and brushes the paint on the canvas. Now what?

Back in university, she was moving coloured papers around to see what would happen with the colours and negative space. She didn't finish the exercise. So she took the sheet of white

bristolboard and coloured paper to her rooms, ripped up the colour paper and glued the pieces where they fell on the bristolboard and splattered black ink over the piece. The professor was ecstatic. Like wow. Wild, man.

70

Angela cleans up the place. Collects her scattered paint tubes and puts them back on the stand. Cleans her brushes. Sweeps the floor. Makes the bed. Gets dressed. Braves the winter cold, taking her clothes to the laundromat where she reads the movie magazines.

In the evening she makes supper and eats alone. She leaves the dishes and reads on the fire escape outside the window which overlooks the back alley where a wino scrounges for food in the garbage bins.

Maybe she'll go to the movie Dr No with Sean Cannery 007.

Maybe she'll write a poem grieving her loss of love. Love is ephemeral.

Like her uncle would say. Buck up.

She starts a self-portrait.

71

Her depression lifts. She goes for a walk in the sun along the river. She should go back to painting landscapes. Plein d'air. Before winter comes. She doesn't know how she gets through the brutally cold winters. As a kid, she skated on the neighbourhood outdoor rink, froze her toes and survived. Not now. She hates being cold.

Good to get outside. With herself, taking in the landscape, not thinking. It's not good to think.

She heads back to her rooms. She is met by Phyllis. We're going dancing. Wanna come?

As I am?

Why not? It's you.

Heath and Andrew and his wife, Judy, are waiting in the car. Andrew has pencilled little moustache with mascara. The college boy who comes from an east-side, respectable family. His grandfather the founder of the slaughterhouse and packing plant. Andrew in his beatnik vestments of sandals and black pants and black turtleneck, unwashed, his rebellion against the empty conformist materialism of his father. The image of the alienated poet who talks about the poems he's going to write.

Phyllis wants to go dancing. Danceland, she says, just east of the city.

So the six of them pile into Heath's car. He drives like a maniac through the streets heading east into the snow falling mesmerizing into the car headlights.

Phyllis wants to turn back. Her thin face rigid, tight lipped. Heath says to relax. She never wants to take risks. Everything safe, predictable, he says.

You could kill us.

We all have to die.

But not today, she says.

The conviviality of the evening is lost.

Heath drives in silence, sullen, determined. There's the Esso, he says. We can stop for something to eat.

He pulls off the highway and parks on the side of the Esso. Phyllis gets out. Heads into the Esso. Angela and the others follow. They find a table. Angela says she's starved to relieve the tension. Between Phyllis and Heath. She wants everything to be okay.

For supper, Heath orders bacon and eggs, pancakes and coffee, black.

Andrew is saying that at a poetry reading, an Indian got up with his hula hoops and danced, chanting how the white man stole the land from the Indians. Andrew was proud that Heath had got up. Bullshit, he said and left the hall.

Phyllis is still in the ladies washroom. Angela goes to see if she's okay.

Why does Heath have to ruin everything?

Heath is Heath.

I'm tired of it.

Angela goes back into the coffee shop where Heath is playing up to Judy, his hand, under the table, up her skirt, while Andrew suffers in silence. Poor Andrew, he can't say anything. Or he'd be admitting Heath is getting to him.

Angela is disgusted he won't fight back. Even if Heath is bigger.

72

Angela hears that a cousin is in the St Paul. She goes to see her and gets lost in the mazes of hallways and doors that end up in dead-ends. On the hallway wall is one of Angela's landscapes. Retracing her steps, she asks for directions. She follows the orderly to Room 320. But her cousin is not there. She died an hour before Angela got there. Brain cancer.

Angela knows about her fiance, knowing she had little time left, married her so she could have her wedding day. In her wedding pictures, she is the beaming bride.

73

Angela finally gets a publisher to read her dirty thirties novel, in which the villain, who was buying up the farmland which the smaller farmers were losing to the banks, is high up in the farmers union. All the publisher said was that his grandfather was big in the farmers union and rejected her novel.

You should revise your novel, Nathan says. Write the story in which a preacher is the villain. You'd win the governor general's award.

I could write about the proletariat.

There is no proletariat. They're now white trash. Like you and me. If you want to get published, you have to be a feminist and write about women being oppressed, discriminated against. That's the big propaganda right now.

From what I hear, it's reality. I took a workshop on getting ahead. We were told the arts are ninety per cent brown-nosing.

Which I'm not good at, Angela says. Growing up, we were told not to blow your own horn.

I'd rather paint and write what I want. Or what's the point?

The arts are run by leftists.

So I should become a leftist.

What's the point if your paintings are stacked in your studio and your writing is in a drawer?

74

Eddie was right. In her paintings, the women, not even women now, but figures like shadows, separated by negative space, flat impersonal, alienated, hollow, without content, lost in a wasteland.

With a glass of vodka, water and lemons, she crawls under the blankets on the bed to warm up from the cold arctic front frosting up the windows. Not good to be alone with her thoughts. Writing and painting is good as they get her into a flow away from thinking too much. Like missing Karl. She knew from the beginning it wouldn't last. It's understandable he's gone back to be with his family.

Back to her painting. Smearing paint on the canvas with her hands like the grade nines. Grotesque masks of women. Blues, blacks, reds. Her reality. Her truth. From growing up. A small child, being sent to the pantry for baking powder, coming back with baking soda. Her mother stomping to the pantry. You stupid idiot, don't you know anything.

Angela sits at the table. She looks at Heath at the end of the table. He is staring at her.

Phyllis brings mashed potatoes and salad to the table. I'll be right back with the fish.

Angela doesn't like fish, Heath says.

I like fish.

Phyllis brings a plate of baked trout to the table. She sits down across from Angela. Help yourself, she says.

Heath fills his plate and passes the food to Angela.

The trout looks wonderful, Angela says.

It's over-cooked, Heath says.

Phyllis wants to know why he had to contradict everything a person says.

I don't, he says.

You have to show how superior you are, Phyllis says.

Angela passes the food to Phyllis.

How was school today, Phyllis?

Same old.

I should have taught the younger grades, Angela says, I'd probably still be teaching.

They come up with the damnest things, Phyllis says. The other day, Patty comes up to my desk and whispers that she peeked in the open door of her grandparent's bedroom and saw her grandpa take off his hair. He put his hair on top of a head on the dresser. Then he takes out his teeth and puts them in a glass of water. I can't do that. It hurts to get your teeth out.

She's going to have to learn that nothing is what it seems, Heath says. He wants to know if Phyllis made coffee.

I'll go get it.

Angela now sees what Phyllis has been telling her, Heath isn't what he seems. He comes across as an intelligent, compassionate man. Being a union leader is a sign he cares about the working class. The exploitation. But he looks down on the working class. His working class wife whom he treats like his servant.

Phyllis has said that, when she first met Heath, he was charming, they did what she wanted, what movie she wanted to go to. He made her laugh. They fucked like minks. It was great. Wasn't long he turned on her. He started criticizing her. She burnt his steak. Which she did deliberately because he was going to say she did anyway.

Even so, she tried to be what he wanted. Went jogging. Got her hair done. Put on makeup. He picked out dresses for her. Nothing worked. She caught herself guessing what he wanted. She felt like she was going insane. She tried talking to him. But he said he didn't know what she was talking about. She was being a drama queen.

Heath wants to know why the coffee is so bitter.

Why are you always dumping on me?

Don't be so sensitive.

75

Phyllis joins Angela in the coffee shop. Thought I'd find you here.

You look terrible.

I feel terrible.

What's happened?

I've left Heath.

About time.

I know, Phyllis says, everybody has being telling me to leave him. But when you're being abused, you don't see it. It becomes normal. You come to where you feel you deserve what is happening to you. You don't want to end up alone. She pushes off a strand of her brunette hair off her narrow face. Her eyes are swollen from crying.

You're not alone, Angela says.

I've never lived alone. I married Heath right after high school. I blame myself I didn't see that I married a narcissist. Everything was about him. What he wanted. How he wanted things done. Order me around. I had to do everything. Cooking. Cleaning up. Make the beds. Do the laundry. I did all the shopping. Ended up being his secretary. Bookkeeping. Paying the bills. Scheduling medical appointments. I never had time to myself while he got to work in his studio after coming home from teaching. And I was still teaching.

He did what he wanted. Which he thought was the natural order of things. Not anymore. I'm done. His alimony goes straight into my own bank account. But I'm scared. I've never been on my own.

He's the one who should be scared. He's never done anything for himself. Doesn't know how.

He'll soon marry a bimbo.

Who's never had to do anything.

I should go, Phyllis says, I'm staying with my parents, but I have to find myself a place.

You have to take care of yourself, Angela says. It's not being selfish.

Listen to her. She's always worried that people are okay. Then she can paint.

74

It's late afternoon. Angela bundles up and goes to buy groceries, see a few friends, stop in a gallery, make contact although galleries have their own stable of artists. She gets back to her place and, tired of winter, mopes about the studio. Phyllis comes by. She says she's had it this time. Heath is so damn wrapped up in himself. Lives in his own little world. What about her? What she wants?

She can't say anything, he gets mad. Everything's her fault. She's the problem.

You don't have to take it from him, Angela says.

Easy for you to say, Phyllis says. You don't know my reality. I've never been on my own. Left my parents, married Heath. He was so handsome, so intelligent. He was going somewhere in his life. But then life takes over. We've drifted apart. Person doesn't even notice. Now we have separate lives.

Angela looks out the studio window into the sunset red behind the dark buildings of the city.

Maybe Heath is right, I've become clingy. I don't want to be alone. I want him home. Drives me crazy he's with other women. Heath is a great lover. He knows what a woman wants. How to get them all wet and bothered. They don't even know it's happening until it's too late, he's got them all hot and bothered in bed. It's the price I have to pay for loving him.

Angela realizes that she's to listen to Phyllis. But Phyllis never listens to her. She brings everything back on herself.

The truth is Phyllis doesn't want Angela for a friend, she doesn't give a damn about Angela. Everything's about her. Her pain. Like with Angela's mother. Angela's to take on her pain. The pain of others. Made to feel guilty if she doesn't make it better for them. What about her? What's she's going through?

You're not going to get mom's approval, Christine says.

She left a hole in us, Angela says. Like I have to get people to like me so they don't yell at me. You fill the hole in you with sex. Feels like you're getting approval.

I don't want their approval, I want their worship.

We all have our delusions.

So we give them what they want to hear about themselves. Like tell a man he's the best fuck you've ever had. But then they want more. They want you to tell them you love them. The fact is that love never lasts. It wears off pretty fast. But while it lasts, it's great, don't you think? You're beautiful. The world is beautiful. Pure transfiguration. Better than any religion. With makeup and the right clothes, we can be whatever we want. It's a billion dollar business. Nobody has to be real.

76

Angela runs into Andrew and Judy in the coffee shop. Angela wants to know if Phyllis is okay. It's like she's gone over the edge.

Don't get pulled in, Andrew says. There's nothing you can do.

It's like she's thinking of doing herself in.

And you have to save her?

I can't.

She's dumping on you to make herself feel good.

Well, it's working because after she left, I felt like crap. I couldn't move.

Andrew says he doesn't blame Heath not going home. Anybody would have to get away from her negativity. Woe is me. Look at the attention she gets. Poor Phyllis having to put up with Heath. Don't you just feel sorry for her. So damn self-important. And you're an asshole if you see the truth about her.

77

Christine says she ran into Jason. Surely you haven't forgotten your old boyfriend. Just so you know, he's shacking up with some girl named Simone. She says you taught her.

Jason doesn't know what he's got himself into, Angela says. She's using him for a place to stay. Soon as she finds a guy with a better place, more money to take her out to the bars she will leave Jason.

And break his heart.

Like you did. Poor bastard.

What's he doing?

He's a lawyer. Criminal law, I think. How are you doing?

Painting.

Good, Christine says. Don't be a stranger. She hangs up the phone.

78

Why tie herself up with a man.? When she wants to write and paint. He'll want to have sex. Go out to see friends. Go to a movie. She never wants to go out. She's writing a short story in which the protagonist falls for the tall blond swimming instructor. His work-out body tanned by the summer sun. She takes him home to meet her parents, her mother a Five&Dime Store cashier and her father a janitor in a nursing home.

After her suntanned swimming instructor leaves, her parents warn her that he's only interested in himself. Calling you Angel-Face. How demeaning.

79

Angela isn't into Warhol with his soup cans and cartoon portrait of Marilyn Monroe. She should paste a sign on a streetlamp with her name and title of her piece, Light of the World on streetlamps.

80

She gives her landlord notice, packs her things in cardboard boxes and moves close to the university. Maybe she will go back and do her masters. Her depression's lifting in the bright, warm June sun.

She stops in the her favourite where she joins Heath and Phyllis.

Been awhile, she says.

The three pack into Heath's car and drive downtown and get drunk in the Senator. Heath goes on his rant against Christian fundamentalists. Like they know what is right and wrong, god told them. As if an atheist can't know right and wrong. He can make up his own. Like cheating on his wife is right for him. They don't mean anything to him. His wife doesn't mean anything to him.

81

In the warm sun coming through the studio window, Angela shapes her clay model of Richard's woman. The high round hips of the eternal woman. Birth mother. Destroyer.

Maybe art comes out of sexuality. The libido. Life force. Maybe she's neurotic. Mad. Creativity coming out of madness. Spontaneous insanity. Her poor, fragile soul corrupted by the expectations and demands of society, life. The need to create order. Make sense of the chaos. To rebel. To be bad. What's the point of being good when life is meaningless? What's the point of anything?

She has to get to work. Concentrate. Focus. She needs clarity, simplicity in her life.

82

Outside the city, Angela sets up her easel on the riverbank to paint the river and the lush green poplar bluff across the river. The sky is ultramarine. She washes the canvas with raw sienna. She sketches in the riverbank, the river, the poplar trees and bluff, lights a cigarette. A warm breeze caresses the tall grasses. She feels safe.

Using cobalt and ultramarine blues, she washes in the river, and for the sky, she mixes titanium white with the cobalt to lighten sky settled on the poplar bluff.

She mixes a variety of greens for the bluff, titanium white for the poplar trees fronting the greens of the bluff.

A clean-shaven old man with his grey hound dog approaches her. I've always wanted to paint, he says.

What's stopping you?

What do I know about painting?

Learn.

Too old.

Never too old. My grandmother, at seventy, started and painted until she died at a hundred.

I'm bothering you, he says.

Not at all.

Out here all by yourself.

So?

In the movies, a woman alone in the trees is not safe.

I have you, Angela says.

83

Angela crawls into a hot bath. She soaks in the hot water, shampoos her hair, gets up on her knees and, under the tap, rinses her hair. Lying back in the tub, she soaps her body in the steaming water, snoozes, gets out, draining the tub. Wrapped in a towel, she blow-dries her mop of hair.

Heath calls. He wants to come over. He hasn't seen her. Where she been?

Busy, she says, working on myself. What do I want to be when I grow up?

Don't grow up, Heath says. Nobody should ever grow up. Grown-ups are awful. Look at what they do to each other. Lie, cheat. Betray you.

What's happened?

You know yourself Phyllis is cheating on me.

No, I didn't know.

It's true.

She tell you.

You know yourself she's a whore.

We're all whores, Angela says. I thought you knew.

You're not a whore.

Yeah, I am.

I don't believe you.

Look, Angela says, I have to get my clothes to my laundry.

He says he could bring over a bottle of wine.

I'm on the wagon, Angela says.

How's a guy to get you into bed.

I'm not fucking you, Heath. Angela hangs up the phone.

He doesn't call, wanting to come over any more.

Men. Fuck. They're all the same. A woman lets them fuck her, they think they own her.

84

Angela is back painting. She works and reworks the canvas. Gives up. Goes out. Walks along the riverbank. When she should be doing her laundry.

She comes back and makes supper, chicken noodle soup. She leaves the dishes in the sink and reads under her desk lamp. A glass of wine would be good. She goes to the liquor board store and brings home a bottle of ShAngelaz, pouring herself a glass and going out on the fire escape where she smokes a cigarette, watching the evening give way to the night.

She goes back inside, has a bath. Wrapped in a towel, she pours herself a glass of wine and opens a paperback of poems. Been awhile since she has read John Keats and the other Romantics. So hopeful things could change.

85

Nathan is having a mid-life crisis. He isn't being recognized for his poetry, which is prairie realism. Not made up reality. Forty below is real. Person could freeze to death. Prairie people know they're looked down on by the so-called sophisticated easterners. So they don't know all the wines. On the prairies, beer is the stable beverage at country dances. At least for me and my friends, Nathan says. And, with the extreme weather, prairie politics are extreme. Rugged individual self-determinism or the co-op collective in which everybody is looked after. A community member gets his share of the potato harvested even though he didn't come out to the potato patch and help. He's not responsible for his brothers even though he's all for solidarity.

It's my politics, Nathan says. And you have to write for the leftist publishers. Aleksandr Isayevich Solzhenitsyn would have a hard time getting published in this country.

You can't stop writing, Angela says.

No, I can't. I have to write. It's sort of schizophrenic. The characters keep talking to me. Telling me what they want said. So they're not forgotten.

86

Angela agrees to teach a painting class for seniors at the community college. Most of them come from paint-by-number guilds. They aren't willing to try anything new. Painting is what they paint from photographs that they have taken of flowers in front of the house. But the classes pay well. And Angela gets to like the old biddies who are happy to paint their flowers and vases. She learns the community gossip, who's teenage granddaughter quit school and deliberately got herself pregnant. What kind of life is the child going to have?

Angela tries to get her students to open up. Their colours don't have to stay inside the lines. Try shutting their eyes and paint.

An old actor, bald-on-top, ponytail, in proletariat plaid-shirt and jeans, unlaced work boots, has no trouble hitting on her. When she rejects his advances, he calls her a bourgeois, repressed bitch. Angela has him removed from the class. He's not happy.

The other male, a retired high school teacher, a John Sevrens, smartly dressed in suit and vest, polished shoes, who is telling her that teachers are being pushed into being more than teachers, they're now being pushed into being untrained counsellors. He walks to the bus stop, waits for the bus. You're so much like my late wife, he says. She too was creative and smart. Didn't really cared much how she dressed. She thought I didn't when she put on her old red jacket, she was going for a smoke. Like I wouldn't smell the nicotine on her breath when I kissed her night. I still don't believe she's going to come in the back door in her red jacket, reddish hair and nicotine breath.

The bus comes and Angela gets home. How does a person manage getting old, the body, brain slowing down. The arthritis. Like her grandfather who had all Tolstoy's novels. Which Angela spent one winter reading.

The next day, her neighbour was told by the city commissionaire to clean up his garbage in the front yard. How did you know about my yard?

I received a call from one of your neighbours.

Who?

That's confidential.

Probably the old bag across the street.

I will be by to see you cleaned up your yard.

I have a truck coming to pick up the junk I'm tossing out from the basement.

87

Angela feels she's not given enough time to paint. As if a bad cold isn't enough, her mom comes to stay for a few days. She takes her mother's suitcase and helps her get her coat off.

I can't believe, her mother says, how you've let the place go.

I'm just getting over a cold.

Her mother looks in the fridge and throws out the lettuce which is going rotten. The milk is sour.

How's dad?

Miserable.

Christine?

Loud and brass as always.

Her children?

She spoils them rotten. I never spoiled you girls. You had your jobs to do. Christine's kids don't even have to clean up their rooms. Mom will.

Her mother puts the washed dishes on a tea towel on the cupboard to dry. She puts on her coat. I'll pick up a few groceries so I can' make supper.

88

Nathan climbs the outside stairs to Angela's studio. He wants to let her know everything's been finalized for her opening. He is puffing from the climb. Angela scrounges on her cluttered kitchen table for her cigarettes. I'm so nervous.

You don't have to be, Nathan says. Everything's been taken care of.

You got a brush-cut.

Got tired of looking after a ducktail.

Makes you look younger, she says.

Ready to go.

The pavement is wet from the cold drizzle. A premonition. She hopes not. She gets in his Volkswagen Beetle. I don't know Angela says, how I'm going to make it through this evening.

A lot of work putting a show together, he says.

She likes Nathan, who's not handsome 'but attractive like Lee J Cobb but she doesn't want to go to bed with him.

89

In the morning, Angela makes herself a cup of coffee. She sits down at the kitchen table with her coffee and smokes a cigarette. Her mother has taken the train back home.

Few people had turned up at her opening.

Even so, Nathan gave a small speech in which he said that Angela is asking if we, as a society, can get over the alienation s into shadows of our own selves. She leaves us with the question: Can we get over our alienation and bring back the community where people look after each other?

There was a short, polite clapping of hands.

A red head comes up to her. You don't recognize me, he says. We took art classes together. Ellard Grayson.

I'm sorry.

Don't be. It's been awhile. I like your paintings. Your layering of colours. Unexpected. When so many are using paints right out of the tubes. I've taken up painting. I have a long ways to go.

Nathan asks if she's ready to go.

Yes, she says.

We will have to go for coffee sometime, Ellard says.

In the morning, Angela finishes her coffee and cigarette, gets dressed, packs up canvases, paints and easel hikes down to the riverbank where, in the sun, she sets up to paint the river and the blue prairie sky. She sits on her stool and lights a cigarette. Here, on the riverbank, thousands of years ago, a young girl came down to the river to get over a broken heart. She was watched by an old crow in the trees behind her, cawing when wolves entered from the trees, stalking her. The old crow protected her from the evil spirits that had possessed the wolves. Angela paints a wolf howling against the full moon in the dead of night.

90

Maybe she can sell herself and make more money than she makes teaching. With the money, she could keep writing and painting. We all prostitute ourselves, even writers and painters, who write for the market to get paid. Free sex. Make love, not war.

Maybe she should become an activist. Be somebody. A hero fighting the fascists. But she would have to join an organization with their hierarchies. Top echelon, then the grunts. Angela doesn't want to be either.

She could write how the male Christian fundamentalist fascists turn woman into baby-factories to fill the ranks of their armies. Christianity is an easy target. Never hear comedians mocking Mohammed. Jesus, yes. They mock him like the Roman soldiers at the foot of the cross.

91

Simone shows up at her door. Angela wants to know how she found her.

Are you going to let me in?

Yes, of course.

I knew you'd haunt bookstores and coffee shops. So I asked around. I wanted to come and apologize. I never meant for you to lose your job.

I wasn't cut out for teaching. Everything's so archaic. A painted tree has a brown truck and green leaves. Like the Fauvists never existed. Don't get your students to try painting abstract paintings. A child could paint abstracts. Never show your students Botticelli's Birth of Venus. You'd get fired. And for godsakes, ban Orwell's 1984, a novel condemning authoritarianism. Do what you're told.

I wouldn't be a teacher, Simone says.

What are you going to be?

I'm taking acting classes.

I love the black fedora.

And the cape?

Yes, and the cape. Very theatrical.

I don't want to be like everyone else, Simone says.

I've never acted. Wouldn't know where to start.

I'm not big in method acting. There is no way an actor can feel the emotions of someone else. She has to create the emotions for the character she is playing. How she delivers the lines given to her in the script. Demur or with an edgy voice. Maybe, growing up, she was sexually abused.

Maybe.

Look, I can't stay, I have classes. But we will have to get together sometime.

92

Angela walks across the Broadway bridge to downtown where she finds Manpower. But she left, feeling uncomfortable that the counsellor didn't even look at her. He stared at her breasts as he talked.

She heads to her coffee shop where she orders a coffee and buys a newspaper. She opens the newspaper to the classifieds. Waitress, Rosemount Restaurant. Apply in person. Finishing Carpenter. Heavy Equipment Operator. Dishwasher. Administrative Assistant. Hydrovac Operator. Aide Operateur sur la route.

Angela finishes her coffee and goes out into the busy street. A young girl in her teens pushes a baby carriage. Angela could never understand why, when they have the pill, teeny-booppers get themselves pregnant and end up bringing a child up on welfare.

93

Women, in front of the federal building in the city, are agitating for women's rights. It's outrageous that married women have no property rights. She can't have a bank account of her own. She doesn't have a choice to do or not to do what she's told. It's outrageous a husband can have his wife signed into an insane asylum. Things have to change. They will. They cannot not change.

94

Angela has recurring dreams where she is trying to get back to where she should be. She's trying to get out of the city. She has no vehicle. So she's walking. She waits for the train to pass, crosses the tracks to the highway going north. There is a lake and cottages on west side of the highway. The highway turns into construction which has been flooded from torrential rains.

Another recurring dream is a rural school. She teaches in the school. But the students chatter to each other and don't listen to her. She can't teach. In another dream, she's in the school gym-size art studio. She is painting humongous abstract painting. She moves the paint around on the canvas. There, it's finished. Down the canvas is solid red. Down the canvas are the letters: She Never Recovered. Like in a country song. In the dream, Angela leaves. She on a corrugated foot bridge over railway tracks in the city. The late afternoon sun is bright and the snow is melting. She feels good about herself.

95

Angela smokes a cigarette on the fire escape. The government-subsidized novel she is editing is a piece of crap. A Christian pastor screwing a married woman from the congregation and getting defrocked. The author is supposedly exposing the hypocrisy of Christians. Why not a novel on the civil rights worker in the news, absconding funds and buying a big house and car, living the good life.

The writing itself is the author showing off she knows a lot of big words used as adjectives and adverbs. Long, run-on sentences. The stiff, cardboard characters play out their roles as villain and victim. There is no way of editing the book. They will have to get someone else.

96

Angela walks to the corner store and buys a pack of Blackcat cigarettes. In the public library, she discovers the nouveau roman, the impossibility of getting reality down on the page. Therefore, a novel is made up reality. But in the real world, life hits a person with reality. Like don't travel in forty below weather. The car stalls in forty below weather, a person could freeze to death. The reality for her is the asshole in the room across from her playing his friggin' drums into night. Or the caretaker, at the bottom of the stairs, leering up her skirt. She is looking for another place as soon as she has the money.

She walks to the corner store and buys a pack of Blackcat cigarettes.

She writes a short story about a husband beating his wife. His kid comes in from chasing crows with his .22 and shoots his father dead to stop him beating up his mom. The editor wrote in the rejection letter that nobody like the husband could be that evil.

97

She makes herself coffee and drags herself to the bookstore. New books have come in so she wheels the book cart and files the books into the stacks. Thank god it's a slow day. A student comes in, looking for Crime and Punishment. He has to write a book review. God, it's a thick book.

You will be glad you have read it, Angela says.

I'm not much of a reader. Why read books when you'll forget what's in them?

You will remember Crime and Punishment.

I guess.

What are you taking at university?

I'm gonna be a sociologist. I want to study why the masses are so vulnerable to propaganda. Like in Hitler Germany.

What about in this country? Why do the masses believe in the myth of the noble savage, our Indians are good, uncorrupted by civilization?

Their language and culture have been taken away from therm.

My parents got out of communist Russia. I lost my language. I'm not a communist. Like my Ukrainian friends. Do you know about the Holodomor?

98

Should give up painting and writing. Get a job, come home, make supper and watch the six o'clock news, an episode of The Beverly Hillbillies. But she can't stop. She has to find answers, why she is the way she is. Keeps her sane. But it's hard to get another show. Maybe rent space and set up her own show. But she doesn't have the money. Maybe if she got a group of artists together. But that would be hard work and take time. So here she is, stacking paintings against the walls around her studio.

She can't think about it. She's not well. The anxiety of ending up on the street. Her life fragmented, disconnected. Like her dreams. Images flashing through her brain like the end of a filmstrip running off the projector. She can't get out of bed. Depression weighing her down.

99

You're Richard, aren't you? I still think of your earth mother. What are you doing in the city?

I'm taking art classes at the university.

As if I wouldn't know.

I have Otto Rogers as a professor.

You're lucky.

You ever been back to Paradise Junction?

Why would I?

Miss Valdenson is principal.

And Gerald? What has happened to him?

Gerald rolled his Mustang. He hit the curve east of town at a hundred and thirty miles per hour. He was dead at the scene. His mother's never got over his death. Never leaves the house. Her husband left her for another woman. What life throws at a person?

But you're okay.

Yes. You?

I'm okay.

We all missed you in the classroom, he says.

100

Angela pours herself a glass of red wine and sits on the couch by the window. A full moon breaks up in the branches of the trees. Jack said he'd call. He isn't calling. She hates when somebody says they'll call and don't. She feels down. The problem is that, if he calls, she knows she will feel great again. It's her need to be liked, to be approved of. Maybe, unconsciously, she still wants to be approved by her mother. For her mother to hold her, say she loves her. Not gonna happen.

To hell with him. Who is he anyway?

She pours herself another glass of red wine. She can rarely afford to buy wine.

101

Angela wants her doctor to give her a pill and make everything go away. He said an antidepressant would help but she would have to work out her own life. How? Her art is going nowhere. She's lonely living by herself. The depression is like lead in her gut. She can't move.

102

Angela was accepted in art camp up north in the trees, getting away from work for a couple of weeks, to paint with other painters from around the province. The famous art critic from New York, Clement Greenberg, would be attending. With Clement's encouragement, Angela experimented with abstract expressionism, the going rage at the time. When she got home, her landscapes became more abstract. She has started using the palette knives to paint the prairie and sky. Sort of breakthrough for her. She was excited about finding time to paint.

103

Phyllis comes to Angela's studio. You seen Heath? He didn't come home last night. I can't find him.

I wouldn't doubt he's in a hospital the way he drives.

He's with another woman.

As if you didn't know.

I can't go on like this.

Then don't.

If you see him, tell him I'm going to kill him.

104

Maybe she suffers from shell shock. Like the soldiers coming back from the world wars. Trouble sleeping. Concentrating. Binge drinking. Ruminating what she could've done. If she hadn't gone with him. The guilt. The shame. Self-hatred. Thoughts of suicide never leave her.

105

How does she get over the rape? She can't blank it from her mind. It's welded in her brain. The shame. The pain. The rage. She's told to meditate. Like the

Buddhists. In a past life, was she cruel to those below her in life? And now she is being punished? AlLife is suffering? Chanting is a distraction. And the moon beams won't purify her. She must live the good life over and over until she gets it right. How? Like those spiritual leaders who have achieved total enlightenment but, in the end, they believe that they become morally infallible. They know everything. So listen and do as you're told.

She's told she has to find her own way. Staying with her own truth. What is her own truth? How does she discover her own truth? What if her truth is that she is not a good person?

How can she be sure of her truth when she can't even prove her existence?

She needs to get out of her four walls.

Somehow, that night of the rape, Angela got herself home. Her mother got up as Angela went straight to the bathroom and ran hot water into bathtub. She tore off her clothes and, in the hot water, scrubbed herself raw.

Why are you having a bath at one in the morning?

Angela shampooed and rinsed her hair. She got out of the tub and dried herself, wrapping her body in the towel and hurried into her bedroom, locking the door. She crawled under the covers and switched off the light.

In the morning she stayed in bed, telling her mother she was sick. Her mother said she had to get up and eat something.

Angela slept, dreaming she is in a house full of people, a large family whom she didn't know. They acted like she wasn't there. She needed to pee but she couldn't find a bathroom. She woke up and went to the bathroom, returning to her bed.

Her mother came and put her hand on Angela's forehead. You have a bit of fever, she said. I should call the doctor.

I don't want a doctor, Angela said. It would all come out and everybody would know she'd been raped. She didn't want them to know. She wanted to see her as she was. A smart, studious young woman.

You should eat something.

I'm not hungry.

Sleep then. Her mother left and closed the bedroom door. Angela dozed on and off. She went over and over what had happened. What had gotten into Jonathan? It wasn't like him. It was like he was possessed. A fiend. He wouldn't stop. She pleaded with him to stop. He was hellbent on raping her. What? That he could get what he wanted. And to hell with her. He had no feelings for her. All this time with him, she was nothing to him. A piece of tail. But he didn't look the kind who hated women. He had a lot of girl friends. How many of them had he raped in his home studio? And got away with it? Christ.

Angela dressed in her housecoat, slipped on her slippers and shuffled into the kitchen and sat at the kitchen table. Her mother told her to go brush her hair, she looked like nobody loved her. Angela stared out the kitchen window into the deserted street. As the sun went down, a silence settled on the street.

Well? Aren't you gonna get a brush and brush your hair? Don't you hear me? What's wrong with you? You're scaring me.

Angela got up and shuffled back to her bedroom where she sat on the edge of her bed. She heard Christine come in the front door. Her mother was telling Christine, there was something wrong with her sister.

Christine came into Angela's bedroom. What's wrong with you? You look a mess. She sat beside Angela on the edge of the bed. Cat got your tongue? You wouldn't believe the day I had. A flat tire of all things. I was late for work. Geraldine didn't believe I had a flat tire. The beauty parlour was busy, busy, busy. A wedding party. I was on my feet all day. You coming for supper?

Angela didn't answer.

No? Suit yourself? I'm starving, Christine said and left for the kitchen.

106

Christine comes to see Angela in the psyche ward. Me and Eddie are gonna get married. Did I tell you? I'm not sure I want to but he wants to. So why not, right? Who else would put up with me? Eddie's pretty easy going. Doesn't say much while I talk a mile-a-minute. Motor mouth. Did I tell you Suzy and David broke up. I'm pretty sure it was David who broke it off. She was always putting him down. Nitpicking him to death. Like she had to compete with him.

Insecure, Angela says.

Aren't we all? Anyway, from what I hear, he's heart-broken. When he's better off without her. Unless she was right about him. He had to be told what to do. He couldn't think for himself.

A lot of people can't think for themselves. They do what they're told.

Like the conservatives.

Doesn't Suzy always have a boyfriend?

Until she got tired of them, Christine says. The bloom of romance wears off and the guys become ordinary. She wants to be with guys who have status. Makes her look good.

Christine fixes her face in the compact mirror from her purse. She retouches her bright red lipstick. We have to get you outta here. The way they drug a person up. You wouldn't believe the gossip I hear in the beauty parlour. The major's son had sex with a minor. He should've been charged with statutory rape. But the family had money. They hired an expensive lawyer who kept him out of jail. I wouldn't doubt, someday, the son gets elected prime minister. So much for justice in this country. Makes me sick to my stomach. Which reminds me, I have a parking ticket. I'll have to go downtown after I leave here. I hate going downtown in rush hour. I'm not good in rush hour traffic. But I do have to stop in a beauty parlour. I'm outta mascara. You'd be surprised how the biddies buy my shampoo and hair conditioner. It's all bottled in the same place. But in different brand bottles. It's like snake oil. But if they want to buy my shampoo and conditioner who's gonna stop them.

107

It is spring. Angela comes back to her rooms from the psyche ward. She stays inside, staring out the window onto the street. A bright orange oriole lands on a branch outside the window. Angela feels her heart warm up. There is life. It's beautiful. She has to stop thinking about committing suicide. Stop wanting to die. The worst has happened. And anyway, she can commit suicide when she can't take any more of her life.

She goes and has a bath, gets dressed in jeans and top and light jacket and goes outside, walking to the park to sit on a bench in the sun. Small children climb up the slide and giggle all the way down. The two boys teeter-totter, laughing with glee. Their mom goes to them. They have to come for lunch. Mom holds a girl in each hand. The boys find sticks with which they shoot each other. Pow, pow.

Angela thinks she will walk to the library on the far side of the park. She has missed being in the library, the excitement of what she could find to read. She doesn't know what she wants to read. Maybe a book on shame. The electro-convulsive treatments left her disorientated. She doesn't know what she wants. Except to get back to herself. Before she was raped.

If only she could get back to painting. Her writing. Why has she lost confidence in herself. She was doing pretty good.

108

Angela shouldn't have come home. What did she think? Her mother had changed? She is still telling Angela what's good for her. She should stay home. What happened happened. She can't go through the rest of life ruminating. She should get a job here and get on with her life. She should go have a bath. You'll feel better.

Angela goes and has a bath. Back in her bedroom, she pulls on a blouse and jeans and goes into the kitchen where her mother is washing dishes in the kitchen sink. Feel better?

Dad on the road?

He said he was going to Pangman, Ogema, maybe as far as Horizon.

Angela pours herself a coffee. Guess I won't see him.

You don't have to go back.

Angela pulls on her jacket. I'm going to walk around downtown, she says.

The streets are icy from freezing over night. From the public school across the street, the recess bell rings and the children file back into the school. Angela had liked school. She liked learning. Not like now, she's crippled by anxiety and dread.

The city bus meanders through the downtown streets. She gets off on Broadway and walks to the bookstore. An old man with loads of white, curly hair is helping a customer find a book in the stacks. Angela waits by the counter. Outside the store window, the street is a stream of cars and pedestrians going back and forth. She sees a friend from university go into the tea room across from the Safeway. She doesn't want to see anybody from the university. She leaves the bookstore and to the bus stop.

That night, she takes the train back to Saskatoon where, the next day, she gets a job in a bookstore on Broadway. She finds a lighthouse-keeping room near the bookstore. That night she sleeps. She is worth something. Two hundred dollars a week.

She gets to work, re-shelving books, helping customers to find books and magazines while Mr Greason is in his office in the back doing the books. He hates doing the books. But it has to be done.

She helps a customer find Treasure Island for her grandson. I wish spring would come, the woman says. She pays for the book and goes out into the dreary street.

A man in his seventies comes into the bookstore. He wants to know if the bookstore has the theatre of the absurd. Angela finds Rhinoceros. The world is absurd, isn't it?

Angela didn't know.

There is no purpose in life, he says. Nothing connects. The absolute truth is that there is no truth. Everybody makes up their own truth. Life is meaningless. So do what you want. In the brave new world, everything is permitted.

He says his name is Harold. He was a journalist with the Free Press. He covered the antisemitic William Lyon Mackenzie King, Tommy Douglas, who wanted to make the world a better place by euthanizing the retards.

I didn't know, Angela says.

A lot we do know. Back in the thirties, Stalin instigated a campaign to starve Ukrainians, millions dead. The newspapers didn't want to believe. Wasn't until 1942, the West learned of Hitler's plan to exterminate the Jews.

Angela feels depressed. She excuses herself, grabs her coat and crosses the street to the tea room where she orders the soup de jour, cream of mushroom and coffee. A heavyset man in a trench coat comes into the tea room. He takes a table in front of the street window and orders a coffee. Behind him, the rain streaks down the tea room window pane.

Angela should know him, the salt-and-pepper hair and beard. But she can't remember from where. Maybe an art opening.

The rain has turned into snowflakes sticking to the window pane.

The waitress takes him his coffee. Will that be all?

He is silent. She leaves while he lights a cigarette.

Angela remembers. He is an art professor. Thomson Beardsley. A Supremacist. Angela has seen his work but she doesn't know him personally. And he wouldn't know her. So she sips her soup de jour.

A big Buick parks in front of the tea room. An older couple get out and come into the tea room. They want breakfast. The waitress tries telling them breakfast is over. The older woman tells the waitress she doesn't like the tone of her voice.

I'm sorry you don't like the tone of my voice, the waitress says. But there's nothing I can do about what you like and don't like.

The older woman wants to see the manager.

I am the manager, says the waitress.

The older woman puffs up and leaves the tea room. Her husband trails after her. She gets behind the wheel. Her mouth is flapping. The old man looks out the passenger window. He sees Angela looking at him and turns away as the car pulls out into the street.

The man at the next table asks Angela what she's reading.

Lamp at Noon by Sinclair Ross.

As For Me and My House, he says, is a classic.

Yes.

I've been always going to read it.

You should.

Do you have a copy?

I work in the book store on Broadway.

I'll have to stop in, he says.

Angela finishes her soup. I have to get back to work.

I'll stop in sometime, he says.

A woman, pleasant-looking, smartly dressed, in her mid-forties, comes into the cafe . She joins the man at the next table. He greets her with a big smile. You look great, he says.

I don't think this is a good idea coming here to see you, she says.

How's John?

God knows.

And Janet?

She's like her father.

The waitress asks if she wants anything. The woman says no. She isn't staying. I don't even know what I'm doing here, she says to the man.

What are you telling me?

I'm tired of having to lie all the time, she says. It's not me.

He sits back in his chair and stares at her. So I'm expendable.

I've dropped your class, she says.

He gets up, buttoning his coat, pays his bill and goes into the street and climbs into his black BMW and is gone.

The woman steels herself for a minute. Then she picks up her purse and gets to her feet.

You did the right thing, the waitress says.

What is the right?

The woman leaves the tea room, jaywalks across the street and, in Safeway parking lot, get into her Volkswagen.

109

After work, Angela trudges back to her room. She should eat but she isn't hungry. She take her towel and soap and housecoat and, going down the hall, she runs hot water into the tub. The last person left body hair on the bottom of the tub. Gross. Why can't people think about other people?

She drains the water and hair. Runs hot water. Baths. Still feels icky.

Back in her room, she makes a pot of tea. Steeps the tea. Pours a cup, adds couple of ounces of vodka. David has gone back east. Nobody gives a shit about her. Not even God. Even her mother cursed her. If you ever have children, she said, I hope they turn out like you.

Better to be alone. People won't see she's a bad person.

Fuck, I'm outta cigarettes.

110

That night she goes out to a downtown bar. The band is loud and the singer is screeching into microphone. He's probably pissed off people are talking and not watching his performance.

Angela orders a rum and coke and, leaning forward, elbows on the counter, she sips her drink, watching the dancers with the band bump-and-bobble on stage like some kind of tribal dance. The dance is whatever moves a dancer makes to the loud drums and amped-up guitars.

Angela can't hear herself think. Which is good. She doesn't want to think. Over and over the same thing. It doesn't go away.

A moustached hipster in a pork-pie hat comes up to her. Wanna dance?

Angela downs her rum and coke and lets him lead her onto the dance floor where they danced, grinding and twisting. She lets herself go and gyrates to the music. She is oblivious of him making his moves. They dance three sets and sit down. He buys her a rum and coke, himself a scotch neat. The hipster says his name is Clayton. He is a jazz musician. Says he has a studio where he teaches guitar. Thursday night is jam night. She should come. He gives her the address of his studio on a napkin.

And you? What do you do?

I'm trying to get at my art, she says.

111

It's the shame that makes her feel rotten about herself. She's worn out, emotionally drained. She doesn't want to feel. She could take hard drugs off the street. Never has. Drugs are not the answer. They'd take over her life. She could end up dead.

She needs a life. Like most people. Get up, go to work, come home, go to bed. Repeat.

Her doctor refers her to a psychiatrist, a Dr Kelly, an attractive woman in her fifties, who peers at Angela over her glasses. What can I do for you?

Angela spills out her story.

That's a lot to carry around, says Dr Kelly. She writes a prescription for an antidepressant and schedules an appointment for next month. She will want to see how Angela is making out.

Angela leaves and, at the nearest drug store, has the prescription filled. Back home, she swallows the pill with water. She prays for relief.

She makes herself a supper of wieners in baked beans with crushed pineapple.

Simone calls. She's been given the part of Chantal in Genet's The Balcony.

I can't wait for the premiere, Angela says.

112

Angela answers the knock on her door. It's Ellard. May I come in?

Yes. Let me take your coat. Would you like a glass of wine?

He takes the wine glass and, at the kitchen table, sits across from Angela.

I like your beard, Angela says.

Thank you. He sips a bit of wine. What is this?

Shariz.

Not bad.

I'm sorry I didn't get to your show. I can't seem to get into abstraction myself.

You know about Rothko's spiritualism.

I have enough trouble with what's here in this world.

Have you looked into existentialism?

You are what you make of yourself.

Other people are hell.

We don't really know other people.

I'd like to get to know you, he says.

Angela pours them another wine. She sits on the couch and invites him to sit beside her. Hold me, she says.

He puts his glass of wine on the coffee table and takes her into his arms.

Being held is nice, she says.

He sits up and picks up his glass of wine. I was wondering if you'd like to come to the Gaslight Coffeehouse Friday night. I'm going to play the guitar and sing a couple of songs I wrote. You could bring some of your poetry.

Let me think about it, Angela says. I haven't been well. Depressed, she says.

You need to get out.

Call me.

113

He doesn't call. Friday night comes and goes. Damn him. She wanted to go. Get out of herself. Maybe it is okay to be alone. She can do what she wants when she wants. She doesn't have to check in. But it is the shits being alone. Person gets sick of herself. All she has are her own thoughts, ruminating about saying no. All about power. Some much violence in the news. Bombings, in Birmingham, Alabama. The Soviet Union having built the Berlin Wall. The on-going cold war.

It's hard having nobody to talk to. But she does fry an egg easy-over and makes toast to eat with her coffee. She pages through the Star-Phoenix. Maybe she'll go see Irma la Douce.

She washes her breakfast dishes, pours another coffee, lights up a cigarette and sets a canvas of her easel. She'll paint a self-portrait to work out how she is feeling. God, if she could only feel better, get back to gung-ho girl back in university. She loved her art classes. Especially the nude studies. She kept piles of them in a portfolio. She paints from them. She should paint a portrait of her maternal baba, who escaped the Holodomor, came to the Canadian prairies and married an Englishman, Robert Stenhouse, a government bureaucrat in the Department of Education. Angela remembered him as being an intelligent, quiet man, who sat in his big chair and read. He was good to Angela, bought her a beret, because she was an artist. She should look like an artist. He was very proud of her. Christine is a scatter-brain but a beautiful girl. She would do okay in the world. Angela would suffer.

She is pleased with how her distorted self-portrait is coming with the blues and blacks with bloody red lips. A harlot from the turn-of-the-century.

Part III

114

Ellard phones. I thought you'd left the country, Angela says.

I went home to bury my mother.

I'm so sorry.

Cancer.

Cancer is a bitch.

Do you have time to go for a coffee?

Meet me at the Broadway cafe . Say seven-ish.

Got you.

Great, Angela says.

He hangs up.

Angela gets home, runs a bath. Her body is so white. She climbs in the tub and washes her hair, rinsing the shampoo off under the faucet. She lies back in the water and soaps her body. She's put on weight. She will have to go to the outdoor pool near her place. As a child, she and Christine, when the family camped at the lake, would go into the water and play like dolphins, plunging into the water, coming up for breath.

She should shave her legs. No. Why? Her aunt never shaves her legs. She has two sons. Her ex drove up and, under a bright sun, stopped in the middle of the street. The two boys ran to the car and got in the back. The car sped off.

Her aunt had remarried. Her husband had said he'd take the boys in as his own. But he ignored them. She thought they'd be better off with their dad. He worked on a ranch in the interior of British Colombia. A number of years ago, the bank gave way and the oldest and his horse fell into the Frazer River. He was never found.

What people have to go through. But her aunt is a trooper. After she divorced her second husband, she taught in a school for unwed mothers.

Angela gets out of the tub and dries herself in a towel. She's going to have to do something with her hair. It keeps getting into her face. Maybe she will get a perm, put some body in it.

She puts on clean undergarments. But what to wear? They're only going for coffee so jeans and plaid shirt and boots. She can't find her beret.

Ellard is waiting for her in the Broadway cafe .

You're looking great, he says.

How's teaching?

It's a bugger. Most students can't reason. You have to tell them everything. And you? Are you painting?

Life keeps getting in the way.

I've got back to landscapes, he says. Sold one for two hundred dollars, can you believe it? But then buyers in the city have a nostalgia grain elevators, railway tracks, false store-fronts, back alleys.

They're not going to buy my self-portraits which expose the anguish in my soul.

Paint social realism. Workers in yellow hardhats.

Except they're looked down on by the intelligentsia who run the galleries.

Paint a woman being lead by a rope by a fat, pompous man in a bowler hat, Ellard says.

Or cat-woman breaking out of a cage.

A superhero of feminism.

That was easy, Angela says. Why didn't I think of it before?

115

The two of them spend time together. After a week's work, they go to the movies. They talk of old times back in high school. How Angela stood out from the other girls. He remembers her correcting teachers. Didn't make you popular with them.

And you couldn't break away from your clique. It was Sandra, wasn't it? She was beautiful with that long blonde hair and great legs.

I thought I was in love with her.

Because she let you fuck her.

She married Steve Conway.

His father was mayor.

Still is.

What has Sandra done with her life?

Five kids.

Good for her.

She should've gone into law.

That's what Steve did.

As she put him through.

I think his father paid for his degree.

So he would come home and look after his father's businesses.

You would've made a good lawyer the way you can make up stories.

Silly me. Hungry? I'm frying beans and wieners. Do you like pineapple?

Not particularly.

I won't put pineapple in. Wanna turn the news on?

Ellard turns on the television, sits on the couch. Attorney General Robert Kennedy authorizes the wiretapping in Martin Luther King's home.

Never ends, Angela says.

Even though, she and Ellard have been spending time together, they haven't had sex. Not until she knows she can trust him. She likes being held though. So, on the couch, they eat supper, watching the TV. news. Later, Ellard makes popcorn and they watch Bonanza.

He likes kissing, which makes her feel like a teenager at the drive-in necking and not seeing the movie. Like the Big Heat. Or From Here To Eternity. God, how she fell for the sultry Montgomery Clift.

Ellard isn't sultry. He's more sulking. He doesn't like teaching.

By summer, she's working in a secondhand book store. She loves the smell of old books. The owner, Sheila Crawford, a large woman in her fifties, is good to Angela. Lets her take books home to read and bring them back.

An old man, in his late seventies, likes to come in the bookstore and browse. He likes to talk with Angela. Says he didn't know he is old until a younger woman told him she wasn't going to bed with him. Women have a prejudiced against old men. They think old men will go senile and have will have to look after them. But I'd probably out last her, the way she drinks and chain smokes. She's young. Nothing will happen to her. She won't get into a car accident. Get cancer. Get old. My daughter, twenty-one, died of brain cancer. Such a loss. She was smart. Could have done anything. Became a brain surgeon herself. Maybe a poet. A damn good poet. Not like we have today, they hate the world, it's not giving them what they want. But they don't want to work for what they get. They don't get what they want, they're oppressed. They talk as if my doctor-daughter is privileged. When she worked hard to get through medical school. Used to be people took responsibility for themselves. Do you think I liked getting up and going at six in the morning to work in the creamery?

116

The Liberals are campaigning on bringing in a new friggin' flag for Canada to appease the French in Quebec who don't want the British Union Jack. There is talk about bringing in non-white immigrants to increase liberal votes.

Diefenbaker doesn't want nuclear missiles from the US on Canadian soil because Canada would become a target of Soviet missiles before the US. The Liberals under Pearson don't see the threat. They want the missiles.

Angela is with Diefenbaker. The bloody, macho cowboys in the Liberal party and their phallic obsessions with bombs.

She's proud that Diefenbaker put in a Bill of Rights. It was a start. Angela was all for the UN Universal Declaration of Human Rights in which the individual is free to decide how they are going to live their life. But the UN declaration has no legal force in Canada.

Beginning of April, she joins Diefenbaker's campaign for the April 1963 election. She goes door-to-door to inform voters of the issues. God, how the fathers of confederation fucked up Canada when they gave Quebec and the Maritimes more members of parliament with less votes. Like Prince Eddie Island, with less than half a million gets to elect four members of parliament. Alberta, seventeen members, with a population of over a million. So much for democracy.

117

Angela wants to know if her dress she has on would be okay for tonight?

You look good.

Not great?

You look great.

You'll be a hit at your show opening tonight.

Hope so.

I know so.

Ready?

I guess so. She gets her coat and pulls on her winter boots.

Are you coming?

I'm coming.

They walk across the Broadway Bridge downtown to the art gallery. He pulls his toque down over his ears. We have to think about how to bring more money in, Ellard says.

Maybe I could bring in money editing stories and novels, Angela says. I could put up posters in the coffeehouses.

They get to the art gallery early. It's a cold night, says the gallery owner. Hope people will come.

Me too, Ellard says. Gail, this is Angela.

Hello, Angela.

Hello, Gail.

You guys didn't walk here, I hope.

Prairie winters are not new to me, Angela says.

Yes, yes, I know. Coffee is being made, Gail says. She excuses herself to greet a couple she seems to know. An art professor from the university and his trophy wife, whom Angela overhears, saying she wished they'd never moved to the prairies.

Angela and Ellard pour themselves coffee. Angela lights up a cigarette.

I wish you wouldn't smoke, Ellard says.

I'm addicted.

You could try to quit.

Tomorrow.

Tomorrow never comes. He introduces her to an art friend. Ben Hershell. He's into pop art. Paints coloured comic strips of lovers in crisis. Droplets of tears down her face.

Ben says that the highfalutin art taught in universities and in museums have nothing to do with our ordinary lives.

So you satirize our cheap, lowbrow lives, Angela says.

I'm being playful, Ben says.

You're an artist, so you're above the masses. You don't have to take them seriously.

You have a show coming up, Ellard says.

This April.

You'll have to see it, Ellard says to Angela.

Sure.

Ben excuses himself and hooks up with a pretty, raven-haired student in a black jacket and slacks and black high-heels.

Angela wants to know how old Ben is.

I dunno. Mid-thirties. Why?

She looks like she's no older than sixteen.

Times are changing, Ellard says.

The gallery is starting to fill up. Are you giving a speech?

Ellard stands in front of the small crowd and talks about his abstract landscapes. The blocks of colour depicting sunrises. Sunsets.

There is light hand-clapping.

Maybe I should go totally abstract, he says to Ben.

On the way home, they stop in a beer parlour to warm up because it's brutally cold as Ellard says. He orders two pilsners. An old man sits at the table against the wall. Is that how we're going to end up, old and alone? The only thing to do is to get drunk?

Maybe he's always been a drunk, Angela says.

He has money, Ellard says, to come in here and drink beer to closing time.

He is wearing a suit under his coat. His face isn't suntanned. It's pretty pale under the wrinkles. His eyes look intelligent. Maybe he is a doctor or lawyer.

I'm going to ask him to join us, Ellard says. He gets up and goes to the old man's table and asks the old man if he would like to join the two of them. The old man gets up, picks up his draft and comes to the table. Ellard introduces Angela and himself. The old man says his name is Zak Protzski. His wife died a couple of winters ago and his three children live on the west coast. He rarely sees them. The grandchildren don't really know him. He's a stranger to them.

Ellard says he and Angela are artists. They're on their way home from his exhibition in the Mod Gallery.

I used to paint, Zak says. A break from the life insurance office. Portraits. Like the German expressionists.

Me too, Angela says.

You should paint my portrait. I will pay you. You could come to my house. It is so empty with Willa gone. I married my friend from high school. We got along wonderfully. She wanted to fix everybody. Our daughter rebelled at fourteen. She didn't want to go to school. She wanted to go out and drink with her friends. Willa suffered. Cindy wouldn't listen to reason. How is she going to look after herself without an education.

My sister is like that, Angela says. Eventually, in early twenties, she got her grade twelve by correspondence. She's a hair dresser and loves to gab with the customers.

Cindy didn't. She's a waitress with two children. She gets by on her looks. She's quite beautiful. But I don't know how she gets through the month. I hope Richard and Denton don't follow her path into adulthood.

We should get home, Ellard says. He zippers up his parka. Angela buttons her coat and puts on her toque and scarf. She writes down her number on a napkin. Call me.

Weeks go by and the old man doesn't call. Maybe he passed away, Angela says. Too bad. I was wanting to paint his portrait. His life on his face.

I have to get to work, Ellard says.

There's something I want to tell you.

What?

I'm pregnant.

You sure?

Yeah, I'm sure.

Do you want to get married?

Would you marry me?

Yes he says.

He heads into the bright sun. Angela goes to get dressed to go to work. She knows she doesn't love him. But he's good to her. And he had a good job teaching. There will be food on the table and a warm bed. She will have to quit her job. Time to paint.

She washes the supper dishes from last night. Sad that Zak died. Very much alive last night, talking about his paintings. Now dead. Person never knows.

Christine calls to say their mom isn't good. She has a pain in her stomach. But they can't find what's causing it. Probably cancer. Her twin sister died of cancer.

How your body betrayals you. You're good, then pow, it smacks you. Angela hopes everything goes well with the baby. She never thought she'd have a baby. But now she's looking forward for her baby to come. She hopes it's a boy. She's been told boys are easier to raise. They sort of boogie along with what they're doing not thinking much about what's going on around them. They have their trucks in the sandbox, play cops and robbers, later baseball and hockey. Then it's love and heartbreak. And country songs.

But, now after they are married, Angela is finding that Ellard has to be right. She tries to say what she thinks of politics, he interrupts and brow beats her, ending up yelling until she can't think. He can't believe she would vote conservative. He'd read about the Frankfurt School who preached that conservatives were authoritarian. He hates Christians. Believes Karl Marx who said religion was the opium of the people.

She gets to the bookstore, apologizes that she is late.

Slackers think they're cool, anti-establishment types. But what if everyone a slacker, nothing would get done, no books to read, no clothes to wear, no food to eat, no surgeries.

I'm not a slacker.

Sheila wants Angela to catalogue the stack of books that have come in. Angela goes behind the counter and gets to work. She doesn't mind the work. It allows her thoughts to wander. She wants to be a good mother. Listen to the child. Help her to make good choices. She, as a child, went to school dressed in uncoordinated top and skirt and odd coloured socks. Christine acted like she didn't know her at school.

Even an ordinary woman is a miracle worker bringing life into the world. A child who will bring good into the world. When there is so much evil. A farmer, his wife, two children, mother are found shot and killed. The farmer's brother is arrested. What happened? How could so much evil seep into a man's soul that a family had to die? Wasn't the first, won't be the last.

Angela can't fathom such evil. There were German soldiers who couldn't stomach and refused to participate in the mass shootings of Jews. Most gave into peer pressure.

What ugly thoughts. Think of something good. Ellard's mother inviting them to Sunday dinner of roast beef with potatoes and carrots roasted in the roaster. His mother is sweet, obliging. Ask and you shall receive. His bald, bespectacled father, a butcher, doesn't say much. He will answer Angela if she asks him a question. Was he in the war? North Africa, he said

Ellard's grandfather had been a rural doctor who made house calls in his 1935 v-8 Ford Phaeton. Often in the middle of the night to deliver a baby, as Ellard's mother, Lizzy, explained. The roads weren't great. In the thirties and forties, even into the fifties, blizzards made for snow-packed roads that took days to be plowed. Lizzy remembered getting stuck in snowdrifts and everybody digging and pushing to get out. In the spring, it was mud and water holes. With paved roads, electricity, central heating, everyday life is much easier. Not to forget washing machines, dishwashers, electric stove.

I'm not who you think I am, Lizzy said. I'm terrible. I knew if I married Ellard's father I would be using him to make babies so I didn't have to be alone all day while he was at work. I could make baby clothes. Even dresses for me as the woman above bakery shop taught me how to sew.

Angela had to say that Ellard wasn't like other men. He helps with the housework like making the bed, vacuum cleaning, supper dishes. Gives Angela time to paint and write. Maybe I'd have time to take singing lessons. Prove my grade five teacher was wrong, I didn't have to mouth the words, I can sick.

118

Ellard comes home late from teaching. He has a couple of students, Cynthia and David who apply themselves to the assignments. The rest think art class is playtime. He says he carries a yard stick which he cracks on desktops to get their attention. He tells them he's not going to jail because he spanked them with his yardstick, he's going to jail because their heads are rolling in the aisles.

You're lucky you haven't been fired, Angela says.

Ellard is upset because Angela hasn't even started supper. Angela is shocked. She's never seen him like this.

I can quickly scramble eggs.

I don't want scrambled eggs.

I can warm up the leftover potato and bacon soup from last night.

Ellard flops on the couch, turning on the television set to watch the CBC news. Walking on egg shells, Angela digs around the freezer for the soup. She thaws the soup under the hot tab and dumps the half-frozen lump into a pot which she puts on the electric stove and turns on the heat.

This isn't the Ellard she's going to have a child with. Where did the good guy go?

I'm sorry, Ellard says. I'm frustrated with students thinking what they have to say to each other is more important than what I have to say about art. Why can't they wait until after school and go to some cafe and find out who broke up with whom. It's the Brook brothers who are the worst. Think they're so cool. Even worse, half the class think they're cool. Given ten years they will be bar-tending in some sleazy bar or moping floors in a old folks home. Both have the gift of the gab. They like to hear themselves talk.

You can't fix stupidity, Angela says.

They can do anything they want, the principal won't do anything. Even the parents are scared of their own children who run around town in packs.

Cowards, Angela says. Even the kids because they don't have the backbone as individuals to stand up for themselves, so they hide in packs. And it's going to get worse. The violence.

119

It's a Saturday in April. Ellard's bulky friend. Peter, stops in for a coffee. He's excited his band, The Sundogs, have been accepted into the July Badlands Folk Fest. Finally recognition after years of songwriting and performing at open mikes and back-alley bars. Their own unique country blues sound. But, he says, Lenore's left the band. I'm gonna have to take over as lead singer.

You can sing, Ellard says.

The songs were written for Lenore.

So write songs for a guy. Like here's your chance to step up to the mic.

I guess.

Angela, get us a beer.

You got broken legs?

I'll go, Peter says.

Angela gets up from the couch and goes to the fridge, coming back with three beers.

I never liked Lenore, Ellard says. Having to be the centre of attention.

She's a performer, Angela says.

But we never knew when she'd go off the notes and sing the way she wanted. There was no way to back her up, so we had to stop playing until she came back to the notes in the song.

I've always wanted to sing on stage, Angela says, but there's the anxiety I'll fuck up.

You have to create a persona, Peter says, someone who you're not.

Like you being a rocker.

Which is so far from who I am.

120

With a few friends attending, February twenty-nine, nineteen sixty-four, Ellard and Angela get married in his studio. It's not long Angela finds she is not used to having another person in her life. Like having to say where she is going and when she'll be back. Another person to make meals for. What he likes and doesn't like. He likes the more expensive brands of food, which add up. Like he has to have Campbell soups. He's not eating bacon, he wants oysters. He has to have Lays potato chips. He buys expensive shirts because he has to look good.

She has to get him to put his dirty clothes in the hamper. She's not picking up after him. She's not his mommie. The worst of it is that he takes forever in the bathroom.

But then she's not perfect. She doesn't like getting out of bed. She hates housekeeping. And she's not a great cook. Christine is the cook. As a kid, Angela got to wash the floors. Weed the garden. Bring in the clothes off the clothesline.

Help
her mother fold clothes. But she had to be told how to fold clothes. Like there was only one way, her mother's.

Angela liked to build things. By collecting scrap wood around town, she moved the stairs from the dining room to the back of the kitchen out of the way. She was more like her Aunt Claire who, after her husband was killed in the Korean war, stayed on the farm. Angela like being outside on the farm, feeding the pigs slop, picking peas and shelling them with her aunt on the porch steps. Her aunt liked her animals. People not so much.

In the late fall, Aunt Claire would come into the city and drop bags of potatoes, cabbage, rutabagas, corn cobs and pails of tomatoes. In the spring, it was Angela's job to break the sprouts off the potatoes.

Life wasn't easy before natural gas and indoor toilets. It was Angela's job to take out the ashes and chop wood. At night, you had to go pee in the outdoor toilet before you crawled into bed. Aunt Claire says she has to pee before she puts her coat on.

And now roads are being paved, power put on farms, life is getting easier and easier. Even so, shit happens. The clutch in the car goes and it costs over a hundred to fix.

121

The next door neighbour, Stan Polowski, is sitting on the stoop, having a beer. Angela goes over and joins him.

Beautiful night, he says. Would like a beer?

I'd love a beer, thanks.

She's heard the story that his wife was the daughter of Dr. Wendy O'Hara. She didn't want Bernice marrying beneath her. But Bernice came home from university pregnant and Stan Polowski, a mechanic, said he'd marry her and adopt her baby. The boy grew up, never making an attempt to make something of himself. First, he took up photography, then he picked up the guitar. He was going to be a rock star, then a writer. He wanted to tell the world how everything was going to ratshit.

Angela feels sorry for Stan who can't be having much of a life with his wife shutting him out of her life. He won't leave her because of his wedding vow till death do them part.

The lights of the streetlamps down the street recede into the smouldering sunset on the distant landscape.

Probably time I changed the oil in your car, Stan says. He rubs the stubble on his chin. Not a handsome man but he has kind, blue eyes. Now in his seventies, retired, he spends most of his time in his backyard garage, working on vehicles, many times not getting paid. He never confronted his customers who never paid of their debt to him. He would say people have enough trouble in their lives.

122

The baby is born March seventh, nineteen sixty-five, a month premature. He's put into an incubator. Angela can lay a finger in the cracks of his head.

Ellard names him George Henry after his grandfather Kinsley. Angela wanted Sean Ellard. But George is good. Beloved. Angela took to him, A warm connection she'd never felt before.

You're so handsome, George.

Ellard drives Angela and George home. He has to get back to school. Angela carries George and the bags into the house. She lies George on the bed. Little stinky-poo. She pours warm water into his baby tub. Gently washes him. Dries him in a soft towel. Pins on a diaper. Gets his little arms into a top. Wraps him into a soft baby blanket. George takes to her breast. Sucks. Her body is feeding him. She is life-giving. What a privilege. She kisses him on his forehead.

When he stops breastfeeding, she lies him back on the bed, wrapping him up in a baby blanket. She sits, watching him sleep. Her son.

She's hungry herself. So, in the kitchen, from the hard boiled eggs in the fridge, she makes herself an egg salad sandwich. She sits down at the kitchen table. Everything has changed. It's no longer just herself. There's George and Ellard to look after.

After school, Ellard collapses in his armchair and reads the art magazine while Angela gets supper on the table.

Supper's ready.

She hears the baby fussing and goes to him. You're awake, are you little man?

She changes his diaper, wraps him back in his baby blanket and picks him up. He hushes. They look out the bedroom window. Chickadees are flitting in the hedges bordering the yard. The children, across the street, are flooding into the school yard, going home. Free time after being cloistered all day. Time to play touch-football before supper. Get home and put on records. My Boyfriend's Back. Puff the Magic Dragon.

As a teenager, Angela was into Elvis Presley. She had his records. His posters were pinned on her bedroom wall. She cut her hair which she wore her hair in a ducktail. She even bought a leather jacket. After a year though, she got tired of pounding rock'n roll and listened to jazz. Been a long time since she has listened to jazz. Ellard probably doesn't like jazz. He's more into country. Abilene. Detroit

City. Patsy Cline's Sweet Dreams. Angela doesn't mind listening to his Patsy Cline records. She is great with that pitch perfect voice. She couldn't read music. But she could follow the sound of the notes. Not like herself. Angela would love to sing. But she wasn't born with the vocal chords. Christine was. She sang country in local bars. She wasn't bad. But she didn't like to rehearse. Rehearsing was work. It wasn't fun going over and over a song.

George is sleeping on her shoulder. She puts him back in his crib. After supper, she pours herself a glass of red wine and sits on the back steps to watch the sun go down. She has to stop feeling it was her fault she was raped.

She drains her wine glass. Pours herself another glass.

123

In the evenings, Ellard works on the the kitchen table, which is cluttered with essays he has to mark, oblivious to her, her reality. She goes into the bedroom and sits on the floor in the clothes closet. They never make love anymore. They did. But it was nothing to write home about. Like it was his duty or something. He was afraid to make love, to feel, as if passion was archaic, beneath him, the commitment. She knows he thinks she's beneath him. The cliche captain of the basketball team, and her, white trash from the wrong part of town. He said she was beautiful. She knew she wasn't. But she had a brain. At first, she wanted to believe he loved her. He was tall and handsome, an extrovert, in control of things, popular. Now, in real life, everything is different. He isn't so self-confident. Things don't come easy to him. He wants to quit teaching. He talks about going back home and working for his father in real estate. He would pick up the guitar again. Get his band back together.

It isn't turning out like she had thought. He had loved her, yes, as long as she did what he wanted. She went along, wanting to feel she loved him.

She lights a cigarette. What is she doing? She'd quit smoking. She goes to the window. She wants out. Before she's suffocated to death.

124

Angela starts making supper when Ellard gets home from school. You picked up milk?

Forgot, he says.

Could you go?

Ellard plops in his chair and picks up the newspaper. I'm fagged.

I'm fagged.

I had to resign from my teaching job.

What did you do?

I brought in books on figure drawing and paintings through the centuries. I got the male gaze lecture. How patriarchy objectifies and control women. School girls have to be protected. And yet in biology, the girls are exposed to drawings of the male and female human body, sex organs. It's called cognitive dissonance.

I probably can get my job back at the bookstore.

How are we going to live on that?

You wouldn't be able to buy expensive shirts we never could afford.

I have to look good.

You're going to have to look for work.

I'm not pumping gas.

Could you go and get milk?

125

It is cold and dark, depressing, as she waits on twenty-second street for the city bus. A cold wind comes off the prairie, cutting through her thin grey cloth coat. There is no money for a new coat. She's worried she will have to go back teaching in some small-town in the middle of nowhere. Not if she can help it. The town people making her into one of them, small minded, repressed, like her mother, who gave up singing, saying she had to be realistic. Her life of church socials and Tupperware parties is being realistic. Angela worries she is more like her mother than she wants to be. Like her mother, she's afraid of herself, of life. Maybe her mother had been raped. Maybe that's why she never leaves the house, a place where she is safe, her life ordered, predictable, dead. No. Can't do that. God, no. Not me. I wanna be alive, feel, experience life. I want to do something with my life.

Angela shivers in the cold wind. Someone is behind her, a presence, she can feel him, his eyes washing over her like a murmuring waves coming off the lake. She glances back. A soldier stands against the grey wall of a department store, lighting a cigarette, his hands cupped against the wind, his dark, smouldering eyes on her, acknowledging her, her existence, as a woman, his serpent eyes, sexual, undressing her. Stop. What is she thinking? But there he is, silent, smoking a cigarette as he waits for the city bus, mesmerizing her in his serpent eyes. She knows she's lost. She will do what he wants. She will go to him, body and soul, giving herself to him, losing herself, her life, in him. He isn't even handsome like Ellard, a pretty boy, pictured on the cover of a harlequin romance. Her soldier is primitive, an animal, yes, stalking her, she is prey to his instinctual lust. In his eyes, she is a desired woman, in heat. She has to stop. It isn't right. It is right. She is beyond right and wrong. There is no right and wrong.

The buses never run on time, the soldiers says.

No, she says, wishing he hadn't spoken, breaking the spell. The cold wind of reality...

The bus comes. She climbs the steps and sits near the front. The soldier follows, a limp in his left leg, the pain in his eyes. She sees the pain and falls in love with him, his suffering, his vulnerability, which makes him a man who would know her pain, her vulnerabilities, her insecurities,and still love her for who she is, not what he wants her to be like Ellard, telling her to get over it and move on.

Her soldier goes to the back of the bus. She refrains from looking back at him. She's tempted. She wants to know that he's looking at her, making her feel like a woman, beautiful, desirable. God, she's acting like a high-school girl never knowing for sure what the look means.

She looks into her purse for her lipstick, laughing to herself, glancing back. He's looking at her, silent, taking her in like he knows he can have her.

The bus stops at where she gets off. For weeks, she can't stop thinking about him. In her dreams, he shows up at her place. They drink and few beer and talk. He says he wants to get back to his photography. She wants to know if he'd like to see some of her pictures she taken over the years. He follows her to the bedroom where she pulls out albums. Sitting on the edge of the bed beside her, he tells her he would've hit on her.

And my perky breasts.

Yes, he says, pushing back a strand of hair that has fallen over her face. She looks up at him and kisses him. She worries about her bad breath. But they fall back on the bed where he pulls up her sweater. As she's not wearing a bra, he nuzzles his face in her breasts while a hand pushes it's way up under her skirt, caressing the inside of her white thighs. She gasps as a finger searches the heat in her body. She climbs back on the bed so he can crawl between legs and come into her. Her body rises to him. She was dead and now she's alive, aroused into life, her blood pumping into every corner of her body, warm, filling her with such a passion she's going to go out of her mind, no past, no future, abandoned in the eternal present.

A rattlesnake has coiled at the foot of her bed, protecting Angela.

– Here ends –

I'm No Angel

Be sure to check out new content from Telostic Publishing, as it becomes available!

www.ingramcontent.com/pod-product-compliance
Lightning Source LLC
LaVergne TN
LVHW090959080826
845145LV00003B/1064

* 9 7 8 1 9 2 6 5 1 5 3 8 0 *